MUSLIMS OF INDIA SINCE PARTITION

MUSLIMS OF INDIA SINCE PARTITION

BALRAJ PURI

GYAN PUBLISHING HOUSE
NEW DELHI-110002

Muslims of India Since Partition

Rs. 540

ISBN: 81-212-0952-8

Published in 2007 in India by
Gyan Publishing House
5, Ansari Road, Darya Ganj,
New Delhi-110002
Phones : 23282060, 23261060
Fax : 011-23285914
E-mail : books@ gyanbooks.com
Website: www.gyanbooks.com

Lassertype Setting by: Rudra Computer Graphics
Printed at : Salasar Imaging System, Delhi

Contents

1

Introduction

Islam has become a major subject of academic studies and concern of international politics. Theories like the "clash of civilizations"[1] anticipated or precipitated assertion of political Islam. Terrorist attack on the USA on 9/11, on the one hand, and the American response to it, particularly in Afghanistan and Iraq as also its conflict with Iran, on the other, have reinforced each other and set a process of homogenisation of Islam.

Decolonisation of the Muslim countries in the mid - twentieth century, boom in oil prices and consequent enrichment of these countries, globalisation and info-technical revolution had already brought Muslim communities closer and made them conscious of an international corporate identity. Perception of a new common threat merely furthered that trend.

There is some truth in the claim of the Islamists that Islam is the most comprehensive religion. There is no field of life on which *ulama* cannot quote references from Quran and sayings and practices of the Holy Prophet, preserved in the form of the *Hadith*, which are supposed to guide actions of every follower of the faith. They assert that there is one and only one Islam which defies time and space.

But what is this one Islam? In Islam there is no Pope authorized to give a final verdict on interpretation of beliefs and practices a Muslim is supposed to follow. While differences over the forms that Islam took in the course of its evolution in the last fourteen centuries and its spread to lands with vastly different cultures may have narrowed down, they have not been obliterated altogether. Moreover, Islam has no religious injunction to terminate its evolution or *ijtehad* (right to innovate in a new situation which is not covered or anticipated in the Quran or the Hadith).

Importance of Micro - Realities

Main hazard of an over-simplified macro view of Islam is that it inhibits a study of micro - realities, which in some cases are more relevant. The American backlash to the Al-Qaida attack on the World Trade Towers, for instance, failed to notice vital difference between ruling ideologies of Afghanistan, Iraq and Iran, three countries described collectively by President George Bush as an axis of evil. The truth is that Al-Qaida had called Saddam an infidel for his avowel of socialist ideology and the Arab nationalism has often been in conflict with ethnically different Iran led by Shia clergy. Failure to take note of the micro-realities is the main cause of isolation of America from not only the Muslim world but also from many of its close allies.

Micro-studies of Muslim communities are, therefore, important for their own sake as also for making more correct generalizations about an aggregate realistic view of the Muslim world. The present study of the Muslims of India since the Partition attempts precisely that. A different community - in terms of its status and role - was born after the division of the colonial India into two entities, India and Pakistan.

Islam came into contact with an amorphous Indian civilization when it came to the subcontinent. This civilization consisted of a series of indigenous little traditions which influenced Islam and in turn, were influenced by it. This process of the two way assimilation created local communities with their distinct syncretic cultural identities.

How these little traditions gave way to a large tradition under the impact of the British rule and process of modernization is discussed in detail in the chapters of this book. Rise of urge for the Muslim identity and the Islamic revivalism in the century preceding the Partition of the country represent the two divergent trends among the Muslims of India under that impact.

Secret of Appeal of Jinnah

Ironically the Westernized modernized educated Muslim elite that was led by M A Jinnah was not well - versed in Islamic teachings and practices. It is this elite that represented the urge for Muslim identity without using a religious idiom. Jinnah treated Indian Muslims more as a nation, than a religious community, which was separate from Hindu nation.

As Muslims were a nation, Jinnah argued, "a nation must have a territory... It lives on the land, it must govern land and must have a territorial state."[2] The new state of Pakistan that he demanded and achieved was not to be religious state as he made it clear in his first speech in the Constituent Assembly of Pakistan.

Religious institutions like Dar-ul-Uloom Deoband, renowned Islamic centre in the Islamic world, also called a *maslak* of Indian Islam as well as religious organizations like Jamiat-e-Ulama and a great scholar like Maulana Abul Kalam Azad were part of the Indian freedom movement led by Gandhi. But religious appeal of Islam eventually could not match the popularity of a non-practicing Muslim leader like Jinnah who appealed to the urge for Muslim identity and empowerment. This apparent paradox of the modern history of India cannot be explained in terms of the current macro theories of Islam.

Keeping in view a broad distinction between religion and identity of Indian Muslims, the issues discussed in this book deal mainly with Muslims and not Islam. Not that the two are completely unrelated. To the extent they are related, the relationship is dealt with by a discussion on the views of Maulana Azad and Dr. Mohammad Iqbal, two greatest Islamic scholars of the twentieth century of India. On the whole, lesson of Indian experience clearly underlines the fact that urge for identity of the Muslims is not only different from religious appeal of Islam but can also be more effective in determining the behaviour of the community in certain circumstances.

A very competent and extensive study of the social, economic and educational study of the Muslim community of India by the Prime Minister's High Level Committee headed by Justice Rajinder Sachar reported that the problems exercising the minds of the Muslim relate to their community and not religion. Even the chief of the RSS has categorically declared that he had great respect for Islam. But its prejudice against Muslims is well known who, according to it, do not conform to its concept of nationalism and patriotism.

However, religion - based identities have their own limitations and can become self-defeating as was the case of Indian Muslims in 1947. In fact no single identity can satisfy all human urges. Muslims must assert, as recommended by the Sachar Committee, their right for a due share as scheduled castes and larger percentage under other backwards classes (OBC's). Their security would also be better assured if they get adjusted as a part of regional and cultural identities. Merely as a religious community, it can become a vehicle of an exclusivist and stagnant version of Islam and isolate it from other communities. All said and done, the Muslims of India did succeed in a significant measure, in managing to face all odds that it faced after the partition due, inter alia, to some exceptional qualities that they had acquired through growth within as diverse a civilization as that of India.

Plural character of India, secular, democratic and federal constitution, independent institutions, free media and a resolute leadership of Gandhi (whose martyrdom multiplied his impact), Nehru and Azad also contributed to preventing a possible fascist backlash.

Not that all the problems of Muslims have been resolved. On occasions their physical safety is threatened. There are many other causes of their discontent. But there exist avenues of protest in which they get support of many fair-minded Hindus. It was not without reason that when Muslims of most nations were represented, in varying degrees, in the terrorist community of the world, Muslims of India were a notable exception, till June 30, 2007 when three suspected terrorists, whose origin to India traced, were arrested, two brothers, one doctor and another an engineer, in Scotland and their doctor cousin in Australia, accused of involved in a failed attempt to blast Glasgow airport. While their doctor cousin in Australia, Haneef, was exonerated of the charge of being involved in the terrorist attempt in Britain and felt proud of cleared of this stigma, the investigation against two directly involved had, till the time of writing this, has not been completed. Even if the charge is proved, it is, in no sense representative of behaviour of Indian Muslims. Firstly, the two brothers are highly educated in technical subjects and beling to Banglore, which might be called technical capital of India. Secondly, they must be in contact with international alienated Muslim community whose anger is directed against the West led by Amercia. They are neither the product of traditional Muslim education like Madrasa in India nor had any grievence against their own country.

Uniqueness of Indian Muslims

Finally the book suggests that Muslims of India, on account of their unique intellectual and cultural capabilities, have the potential of becoming a great national asset and of playing a crucial role in relieving the Muslim world of the unprecedented crisis that has gripped it. International scholars of Islam have not done enough justice to the uniqueness of the character of Muslims of India and the complexity of the problems they have tackled. To that end, this book attempts to make a humble and, perhaps, some original contribution.

The book primarily deals with the post-partition problems concerning the Muslims of India from time to time. References to the pre-partition days and to Islam are made only to the extent they are relevant to their present.

It is a collection of articles published in newspapers and journals at different times and on various aspects of the Indian

Muslims, the articles have been edited and updated to avoid repetition to the extent possible and to retain their contemporary relevance.

References

1. Title of a book written by Samuel P. Huntington, Penguin Books.
2. Speeches and Writings of Mr. Jinnah ed. Jamil-ul-din Ahmed, Vol. I, p. 236, Lahore.

2

Indian Muslims since Partition

The title of this paper may well have been Indian Muslims since Independence. But the present title underlines the crucial impact, on Muslims, of the partition of the country. For in reality it marked a division of the Indian Muslims, first in two and later in three nation states; whereas the bulk of the Hindu community (and of other non-Muslim communities) was consolidated in what remained of India, retaining its historic and civilisational continuity.

1

Partition and After: Early Years

The idea of Pakistan, as is well known, had little support in the areas that now comprise that country. Its battle was fought essentially by those Muslims who lived in the Hindu majority areas, which remained a part of India. Iqbal, who is credited with the authorship of the idea, wanted to apply it to the Muslim majority areas of the subcontinent. In a letter to M A Jinnah, dated June 17, 1937, he asked, "Why should not the Muslims of NW India and Bengal be considered as nations entitled to self-determination?" But while suggesting establishment of Islamic states through the division of the country, he categorically advised Jinnah "to ignore Muslim minority provinces". He further urged him to concentrate on the Muslims of the north and west of India.[1]

But the Muslim League leadership ignored this advice and found it easier to work upon the sense of fear and insecurity of Muslims in Hindu majority areas. It was able to persuade the Muslims that a separate Muslim state on either side of India would be a better guarantee of their rights.

Trauma

But soon after the partition, the entire Muslim League leadership, which had a popular base, left India along with most of the administrative, social, cultural and intellectual Muslim elite for the new, greener Islamic pastures, leaving Indian Muslims leaderless and impoverished.

For Indian Muslims, August 15, 1947 was the gloomiest day of their history. "What the Muslim community got out of independence and partition was a sense of insecurity, frustration and uncertainty."[2]

The trauma of the Muslim community after the partition is often compared with what it suffered at the time of the collapse of the Mughal empire. But at that time, the community retained its self-esteem and good-will of its compatriots. This is borne out by the fact that a Muslim king was accepted by the whole nation as a symbol and leader of the first war of independence in 1857. Moreover, the presence of British power ensured that Muslims were not discriminated against.

But in 1947, the Muslims could not bank on a third power and lost much of the respect of the majority community for the role some of them had played for the disintegration of the country. In terms of their self-confidence, prestige and role, the Partition marked a break in the 800 years of Muslim history in India. In many respects, it was a birth of a new community.

The community received no guidance from its erstwhile leaders except a counsel of despair, resignation and withdrawal.

The Muslim League leaders, while migrating to Pakistan, just bid "Khuda Hafiz" to their former followers in India those who remained behind became irrelevant for them.

Reversal of communal tide

It was Maulana Abul Kalam Azad, "the lonely and tragic figure of Muslim politics",[3] who provided beacon light in this hour of darkness. In a touching and inspiring speech in Delhi Muslim convention on November 4, 1947, he called upon the Indian Muslims "to take the pledge that this country is ours, that we belong to it and that fundamental decisions of its destiny will remain incomplete till we participate in them". There is no place, he declared, "for either cowardice or frenzy in a Muslim"[4]

Maulana's status in the freedom movement and in the government of India made him a source of hope and confidence for the Muslim community.

Two more factors had a decisive impact on the communal situation in the country. Accession of the Muslim majority state of Jammu and Kashmir to India on October 26, 1947 stemmed and reversed the anti-Muslim tide in north India. Gandhi's martyrdom on January 30, 1948 was another decisive blow to the communal hysteria. In addition, Nehru's determined leadership consolidated the secular democratic basis of the Indian state.

The partition did cast its shadow on the process of Constitution making. The traditional Muslim demands for reservation in jobs and legislatures, proportional representation, etc, were voluntarily withdrawn by the Muslim members of the constituent assembly. They ungrudingly accepted Hindi as the official language of the country without pressing the claims of Urdu or Hindustani. The partition also strengthened the case for a strong centre and against provisions for decentralization and genuine federalism lest they should further threaten the unity of the country.

However, the founding fathers of the Indian Constitution provided for fundamental rights and minority rights which constitute the essentials of the principles of secularism and democracy. It was flexible enough to make room for checks on centralising tendencies and for empowerment of the regions later. According to the noted constitutional authority D D Basu, "the sum total of the constitutional provisions make our state more secular than even the US."[5]

Achievements of India in early years of independence such as embarking on a planned development, laying foundations of democratic institutions, building an administrative edifice, ensuring internal stability and acquiring an international status owed a lot to its adherence to the basic principles of secular democracy and, in turn, strengthened the faith of its people in these principles.

India's goodwill in the West Asia, symbolized by personal friendship of Nehru with Nasser, which isolated Pakistan in the Muslim world, was a more tangible dividend of secularism and a matter of pride for Indian Muslims.

Role of ideology in the post-independence India also undermined communal polarization. For political parties in the 1950s were broadly formed on ideological basis, with the Congress on the left of the centre and the socialists as the main opposition. Other ideologies of the political spectrum included Marxism of the Communist Party, liberal capitalism of the Swatantra Party, and at the margin militant nationalism of the Bhartiya Jana Sangh. There was no important party, except the Muslim League in Kerala and the Akali Dal of Punjab, which excluded members of the other communities from its membership.

Another factor that discouraged community based identities in that period was the resurgence of regional identities, followed by linguistic reorganization of the country in 1956.

Not that the Muslims did not have any problems in this period. But their expectation were low and fears high. The system offered more than they expected and was less hostile than they feared. Pakistan's comparatively poor performance in foreign affairs, functioning of democracy, and industrialization, too, inspired better confidence in Indian Muslims in the system of their country.

How far did the promises of the 50s, the decade of triumphant secularism, materialize?

The later development indicated that they were no less illusory than were the prophecies of gloom in 1947.

II

Assertion of Self-identity

Gradually, the Muslim mood of withdrawal and resignation gave way to consciousness of rights, assertion of identity and protest against perceived injustices. A number of developments were responsible for this transformation.

During the decade of 50s, the Muslims lost three stalwarts among their leadership. Maulana Abul Kalam Azad and Rafi Ahmad Kidwai died, while Sheikh Abdullah was put under indefinite detention for allegedly conspiring to bring about Kashmiri secession from India. Azad's interpretation of the Quran and Islam had provided religious sanction to the concept of composite Indian nationalism. Kidwai, as a fine specimen of Ganga-Yamuna culture, could communicate with non-Muslims through a common idiom, Hafiz Ibrahim and MC Chagla who replaced Azad and Kidwai in the union cabinet could give neither religious nor cultural expression to Muslim aspirations.

Abdullah had demonstrated the confidence of the Muslim community in the secular polity of India as also the tangible benefits of secularism to Indian nationalism. His arrest made many Muslims wonder why even Abdullah was not trusted in India. With his arrest, Kashmir, which had played a crucial role in reversing the communal tide in 1947, became, in later years, a factor in the revival of communalism in the country.

Azad, Kidwai and Abdullah not only inspired self-confidence in the Muslim community but were also effective inter-community bridges. In their absence, the cause of inter-community understanding suffered.

Leadership Vacuum

At organizational level, the leadership of the Muslim community, after the partition, was thrust upon Jamiat-ul-Ulema Hind, an ally of the Congress Party. But it continued to suffer from the inadequacies on account of which it had lost the race for Muslim leadership to the Muslim League before the partition. Muslim political and cultural aspirations could not fully fit into its theological strait jacket. The Jamiat's concept of nationalism as a contract between Hindus and Muslims-on lines of the Madina covenant that the Prophet of Islam had forged between Muslims and non-Muslims to form a common community at Madina-no longer impressed Hindus after the Muslim demand for a separate state had been conceded. The Jamiat was all along an appendix of the ruling Congress Party, through which the latter sought to consolidate its vote bank. The Jamiat thereby acquired an image of a sarkari party and was as such incapable of representing anti-establishment sentiments which were bound to exist, in some degree, among the Muslim as they did in any other community. But these sentiments could not get an adequate expression in the then prevailing one-party-dominant system in the country. Conscious of its limitations, the Jamiat sought to broad-base its activities and took the initiative in convening an all-India Muslim convention in June 1961. It excluded what were called communal parties like the Muslim League and the Jamaat-e-Islami. But a group of the Jamiat-ul-Ulama, led by Mufti Atiqur Rehman, publicity favoured co-operation with the Jamaat. The convention was further split on a resolution of the communist leader ZA Ahmed aiming to ban communal parties.

All in all, the gap left vacant by the Muslim League, as a consequence of the partition, and due to the absence of Azad, Kidwai and Abdullah could not be fully filled by the Jamiat or any coalition of Muslim parties or any secular party. Muslims, thus, lacked not only adequate articulation but also a communication link with the Hindu majority.

Perhaps the first communal riot, which took place in Jabalpur in Madhya Pradesh in 1961, after more then a decade of communal peace reflected this basic deficiency of the Indian polity at that stage rather than a mere aberration caused by a local event. The fact that a Hindu girl of a 'bidi' manufacturer eloped with a Muslim boy of another bidi manufacturer could cause a sense of humiliation in the Hindu community and that the two communities had developed business rivalry due to competition of two bidi manufacturers merely indicated lack of trust between the two exclusive communal alignments.

Nehru was still the most effective inter-community bridge. He was shaken by the Jabalpur riot and renewed his offensive against communalism. He also set up the National Integration Council. However, the upsurge of patriotism among all communities following the Sino-India war of 1962 led the Asoka Mehta committee, appointed by the council for suggesting measures for national integration, to declare that its role had become redundant.

The euphoria over national integration was rudely shaken by the chain of communal riots in 1964 at Jamshedpur and Rourkela. But their epicentre significantly lay in the valley of Kashmir. Already agitated against a regime of corruption and repression imposed on them through rigged election[5] and detention of popular leadership, Kashmiri Muslims were enraged over the theft of a holy relic (sacred hair of the Prophet) from the Hazratbal shrine in early 1964. The reports of the suppression of the angry masses, including police firing on them, had a backlash in Dhaka, the capital of the then East Pakistan. A chain reaction of anti-Muslim riots within India followed thereafter.

Post-Nehru Era

The riots jolted Muslims of India into a radical rethinking of their role. The riots were cited as one main reason for convening what was called the Muslim Majlis-e-Mushawarat at Lucknow on August 8-9, 1964. It was convened by a veteran Congress leader Syed Mahmud at the initiative of a former socialist leader A J Faridi, and was attended by about 80 Muslim leaders belonging to different schools of thought from all over India. In his address, as chairman of the reception committee, Faridi said: "Since independence, Muslims had almost retired from politics. But what happened in the two decades that followed showed that it was not a wise decision".[6]

Though the Mushawarat was merely a coordinating body and not a political party, it was the most significant development in the Muslim politics of India after the death of Nehru and indicated decline of trust of the community in the post-Nehru leadership. It marked the first effective self-assertion by Muslims. In a way, Nehru era had ended before his death in May 1964. after India's humiliating defeat by China in 1962, he had suffered a political, mental and physical setback from which he never recovered. The incidents in Kashmir and the reactions to them had taken place when he had been publicly declared to be ill.

Some more developments in the post-Nehru era adversely affected the Muslim mind. The new government at the centre took measures for the forced constitutional integration of Jammu and Kashmir with the union of India in the teeth of opposition of the Kashmiri Muslims. Changes in the nomenclature of the head of the state and of the government, the change in the status of the former from being elected by the state assembly to being nominated by the president of India, extension of emergency provisions of the Indian Constitution of the state, and conversion of the regional National Conference to a branch of the Indian National congress created an unprecedented wave of anger in Kashmir which tempted Pakistan to send armed infiltrators into Kashmir leading to Indo-Pak war of 1965.

Though Sheikh Abdullah had ceased to be a hero of Indian nationalism since 1953, the ideological umbilical chord between the Kashmiri nationalism and the Indian nationalism, led, respectively, by him and Nehru, was not cut during the Nehru era. But after him, the integrationist measures of 1964 and 1965, Kashmiri Muslim bitterness against India reached new heights; it eroded their ideological affinity as well.

The Indo-Pak war in 1965, following the developments in Kashmir, was another crucial impact on the Muslim situation. It was a war between two nation states which established, as nothing had done before, the position of Indian Muslims as part of the Indian nation. Their participation in and contribution to the war effort, symbolized by Havaldar Abdul Hamid, who was posthumously honoured with the highest military award of Param Vir Chakra, added to their confidence in their Indian identity.

But the war also brought into sharp focus the perennial controversy over the Muslim attitude towards Pakistan. For, most Muslims could not match the intensity of hatred of an average Hindu towards the national enemy. This fact prepared the ground for a whisper campaign against Muslims in general and the Muslim dignitaries at the highest positions in particular, casting aspersion on their loyalty and patriotism.

Some people, of course, took a more sympathetic view of the Muslim mind on the subject. Commenting on this controversy, eminent journalist B G Verghese concluded: "It was probably true that some or many Indian Muslims had a feeling of sympathy towards Pakistan and wished it well. But it hardly constitutes a charge of disloyalty"[7]. The veteran former communist leader BPL Bedi asked in the same vein: "Why should it be expected at all of any Indian Muslim to prove his loyalty to India through his enmity of Pakistan?" He asserted that "there was nothing inconsistent in an Indian Muslim being at heart fully and totally loyal to India and a well wisher of Pakistan".[8]

But most of the Hindus would not take such a generous view. They rarely drew a distinction between trans-national affinities and extra-territorial loyalty. Representing the other end of the political spectrum, the then Jana Sangh leader A B Vajpayee asserted: "It is a fact that many Muslims find Pakistan dearer than India and Al-Aqsa nearer than Jagan Nath". Those who felt alienated he said, "are free to leave the country."[9] Anti-Pakistanism almost became a litmus test of loyalty to India, in particular for Muslims who had not been forgiven for their alleged role in the vivisection of the country in 1947.

Shedding the guilt

However, after 1965 the reaction of the Muslims to this view was no more apologetic. The post-independence generation was not loaded with a sense of guilt for the creation of Pakistan and refused to be answerable for the sins the previous generation was supposed to have committed. In fact, some fresh evidence and theories were cited to prove that the Muslims alone could not be blamed for the partition. Maulana Azad, for instance, in his book *India Wins Freedom*, especially the part that was released thirty years after his death, holds Congress leaders, including Nehru, equally responsible for it. In a more strident tone, the Jamaat-e-Islami's official organ Radiance editorially asserted: "post-independence Muslim is not prepared to listen to any non-sense with regard to his or his parents' role, if any, in the partition, for which, according to authentic history, Sardar Patel, Jawaharlal Nehru and Mahatma Gandhi were primarily responsible."[10]

Thus started a new phase of assertion by the Indian Muslims of their Indianness as well as Muslimhood. They no longer suffered from the schizophrenic panges of the previous generation caused by claims of dual identity. They insisted on simultaneity of their Indian and Muslim identity. It was the awareness of the former that enabled them to shed all inhibitions in asserting their perception of Muslim identity and interests. They tended to believe that their right to assert themselves flowed from the fact that they were equal citizens of the country.

Many instances can be cited of the twin processes of indigenisation and assertiveness of the Indian Muslims in this period. Many Muslim communities started searching their indigenous roots. Some of them were able to trace their ancestry to the tribes of Ramayan and Mahabharat, instead of the foreign Muslim countries as used to be the fashion so far. The growing popularity of the Bareilly school of Islamic learning as against the Deoband school indicated the same trend. For, the former permitted worship to tombs and 'ziarats' of local 'faqirs' and saints, which in a way is confirmation of attachment with the soil.

Symbols of Muslim Identity

So far as Muslim assertion is concerned, it was pronounced on three main issues which emerged as symbols of the Muslim identity, namely, Aligarh Muslim University, Urdu Language and Muslim Personal Law.

On May 20, 1965, the president of India promulgated the Aligarh Muslim University (Amendment) Ordinance which was enacted by parliament in its autumn session. It reduced the court of the university to an advisory body, to be wholly nominated by the government. And it appointed a visitor with wide powers. The amendment was intended to bring the AMU at par with other central universities. An earlier attempt to drop Hindu and Muslim words from the names of the Banaras and Aligarh universities, respectively, in order to de-emphasise their communal character, was abandoned due mainly to the opposition of the Muslim community. The new attempt to change the minority character of the Aligarh university alone met with greater opposition of the community.

The status of Urdu in UP and Bihar states also became a live issue. For, though Muslims reconciled to the displacement of Urdu from its pre-eminent position of pre- independence days in view of the changed political situation, they aspired for at least a second language status for it.

The case of Urdu is often presented on the basis of secular arguments as it is claimed to symbolize a composite culture. But the fact is, observes Muhammad Qamaruddin, that "a Muslim's love for Urdu is only second to the regard for his religion".[11] Similarly, discussing the fate of Urdu in India, W C Smith opines: "The Indian Muslim community is in danger of being deprived of its language, than which only religious faith is a deeper possession."[12] Thus, though, there were many eminent Hindus among the 22 lakh signatories to the memorandum demanding rightful status for Urdu to the president of India, Rajendra Prasad-it reflected the innermost urge of the Muslim community, particularly in north India (for a fuller discussion to the role of Urdu, see chapter 7, Urdu and Muslim Identiy.)

The third symbol of the Muslim identity, namely, the Muslim Personal Law, was soon to become the most explosive communal issue. As JDM Derret had warned in 1968: "If there is a frontal attack on the Personal law in India, it will survive with a tenacity it has been unable to show in countries where the majority of the population are, and always have been, Muslims."[13]

It is true that with the proliferation of educational institutions all over the country increasingly a smaller percentage of Muslim students is dependent on the AMU for its educational needs. With the growth of regional language and identities, lesser number of Muslims need Urdu for self-expression. With the increasing awareness among women about their rights, and with the growth of the present socio-economic conditions, polygamy and some other provisions of the Muslim Personal Law have become obsolescent. But it is futile to argue against the utility of these symbols. For, a community adopts such symbols not out of a rational choice but under a certain combination of circumstances. In the case of Muslims, they emerged as a manifestation of their urge for identity.

The exclusivist trends in this urge were encouraged by the ambition of some leaders of the community to project it as the balancing force in a politics polarized between a weakened Congress and the united opposition in 1967. The Jammat-e-Islami organ *Dawat* quoted S W Hussain to assert that "there were not two (Congress and opposition) but three forces in the country; the third being the Muslims".[14] But the ambition of building a solid Muslim block balancing and dominating national politics was obviously too unrealistic to materialize and merely provoked the majority community to close its ranks at many places.

The assertive phase of Muslim politics witnessed communal tensions and riots. Starting from Jabalpur (1964), there were 3,646 riots in various parts of the country, in some cases for the first time, culminating in Gujarat, the state of Gandhi's birth, in his centenary year of 1969, taking a toll of 674 human lives, the worst till that date since the partiton.[15]

Clash with nationalism

In the 70s the Muslim community became further out of tune with the nationalist sentiments during the Bangladesh movement. Excepting the Bengali Muslims, the Muslim community felt culturally and emotionally closer to what was then West Pakistan.

Meanwhile, Indian nationalism, under the leadership of Indira Gandhi, hailed as an avtar of goddess Durga by the then Jan Sangh leader Atal Behari Vajpayee, acquired more strident and masculine character; it felt encouraged by the two victories against Pakistan (and its split), the annexation of Sikkim, and a nuclear explosion.

While for Mahatma Gandhi, Indian nationalism was a means for the attainment of a higher moral objective, and while Nehru formulated the demands of national interest in a moral idiom, Indira Gandhi's concept of nationalism was amoral and an end in itself. She aspired for role for India on the basis of merely its physical strength, for which, she believed, solid support of the whole nation without dissent was necessary. Nationalism thus got differentiated from patriotism and political values like freedom and democracy became subordinate to it.

There were also some other political factors that contributed to the emergence of this situation, for example the imposition of the emergency in the country in June 1975 against which Jayaprakash Narayan led a revolt. Muslims felt as suffocated during the emergency regime as any other community and by and large supported the Janata Party in over-throwing it in the general elections of 1977.

For a while Congress-Janata polarization replaced the communal divide of the Indian politics. As co-sufferers of the emergency and availing the opportunity for a dialogue in jails, the RSS and Jamaat-e-Islami leaders developed mutual cordiality and exuded a fresh optimism about Hindu-Muslim relations. The basis of their dialogue was not made public. But in keeping with their known stand, the scope for evolving a community-based (instead of region-based) federal polity was perhaps explored. But it did not make much headway on account of the obvious impracticability of the idea.

Another hopeful pointer was the willingness of the RSS to consider JP's advice for allowing non-Hindus, including Muslims, into its fold. The erstwhile Jan Sangh, after its merger with the

Janata Party, accepted all the secular formulations of the latter. Fresh initiative to improve Indo-Pak relations and the first fair election in the history of Kashmir, that went a long away in reviving the confidence of its people in Indian democracy and about their future therein, had a salutary effect on the communal climate in the whole country.

However, the Janata coalition, that JP had cobbled up together and had been cemented by anti-Congressism, collapsed under the weight of its own contradictions. JP regretted that "the RSS did not implement his advice despite assurances to open its doors to Muslims."[16] The issue of the dual membership of the RSS followers in the Janata Party led to its split and the return to power of Indira Gandhi, in the elections of 1980, with the slogan of a strong nation and a strong government. She was accused of playing the Hindu card in the election campaign. Her frequent visits to Hindu shrines and religious personalities gave her a religious image. But what really endeared her to Hindu militants was her militant nationalism, which she first introduced in Indian politics in early 70s and which tended to fill in the ideological vacuum to which Indira-JP confrontation had significantly contributed as none of the sides was ideologically based. Indira's no non-sense attitude towards foreign powers and ethnic and religious minorities within the country reflected a militant nationalist mood.

Her refusal to condemn entry of Soviet forces into Afghanistan, which aroused indignation of the Muslim world, the projection of Pakistan as a source of threat to India's security, and the reference to the possible role of the Gulf money in the conversion of the scheduled castes of Meenakshipuram to Islam in 1981 appealed to those Hindus who were scared by the resurgence of Islam outside and Muslim assertion within the country. The dismissal of the Akali-led government in Punjab in 1980, the army action at the Sikh Golden Temple at Amritsar in 1984, and the dismissal of the duly elected governments of Farooq Abdullah in Kashmir in 1984 by engineering defections on the ground of his alleged anti-national role, enabled Indira Gandhi to satisfy the militant nationalist sentiments of the Hindus.

The controversy over whether she became a staunch Hindu or a staunch nationalist is irrelevant, for the dividing line between Hindu communalism and the extreme form of Indian nationalism is rather blurred. The majority everywhere tends to assume the right to define the parameters of nationalism. But in India's case, Hinduism is not merely another religion but a representative of the ancient and native heritage.

It is on account of this conceptual ambiguity about Indian nationalism that it does not evoke the same degree of emotional response from all communities of India. How could Muslims, for instance, worship Bharat Mata, Ram and Krishna even though they might have reverence for them? For, "Muslims particularly being non-idolatrous, are conscience-bound not to entertain any such loyalty that places them against God",[17] Nor does an average Muslim share the degree of hatred for Pakistan that has become a second nature with many a Hindu nationalist.

Nationalism in India's case has never been a unifying force; not even when it was tempered with Gandhian compassion and Nehruvian sophistfication. As Jinnah's remedy proved worse than the disease, Muslims in India had reconciled to Indian brand of nationalism. But the crude and militant phase of Indian nationalism which prevailed in India in the 80s after the second tenure of Indira Gandhi made fresh demands of conformity and uniformity which minorities, including Muslims and Sikhs, were unwilling to accept.

This phase of Indian nationalism coincided with what was called the Islamic wave, triggered off by Khomeini revolution in Iran, in 1979-80. the ripples of this wave crossed over to the Indian borders which further encouraged the Muslim assertion that was rising due to autonomous indigenous factors already discussed.

III

Consolidation of the Hindu Communal consciousness

The era of Indira Gandhi continued beyond her death with added vigour. Her 'martyrdom' consolidated the bulk of the Hindu community in a manner rarely done before. The largest ever margin of victory of the Congress Party in the elections of 1984 reflected the consolidation of the community. But it was also more sharply divided from other communities than ever before.

Sharpest divide

A sharp-in fact the sharpest ever-communal divide till date-emerged after the judgement of the Supreme Court on the celebrated case of Shah Bano when the demand of conformity and uniformity ferociously clashed with the Muslim urge for identity. On April 23, 1985, the chief justice granted maintenance to the Muslim women from her separated husband under Section 125 of IPC which is applicable to all communities. It was followed by never-ending protest rallies all over the country by the Muslims.

The way the government of India handled the issue worsened the situation. After presenting a stout defence of the Supreme Court judgment on the Shah Bano case, it agreed to enact the Muslim Women (Protection of Rights on Divorce) Act in 1986 on the lines suggested by the Muslim leaders. It caused a strong backlash among the Hindus, including the liberals among them, who condemned the government for its "abject surrender to Muslim fundamentalism". Most of the backlash was consolidated by the BJP. Its leaders justified the resurgence of Hindutva as a logical reaction to the Shah Bano episode which, according to them, exposed Muslim reservations about joining the mainstream and the government policy of appeasement of the Muslims.

It is widely believed that in order to neutralize the Hindu backlash, the government arranged to get the gates of the sanctum of the Babri masjid opened to allow worship of the idols that had mysteriously appeared there in 1949. The stay order in the case was got modified at the level of a junior judicial officer. This action provoked fresh wave of protest among the Muslims. The rally on March 30, 1987 at the Boat Club, New Delhi, was the biggest Muslim rally in the country since independence. As a further attempt to win back Hindu support, the Congress government of UP permitted 'shilanyas' (foundation stone laying ceremony) of the Ram temple, on the eve of the elections in 1989, within the parameters of the disputed land. Rajiv Gandhi started his election campaign from Ayodhya with a promise to usher in a Ram Rajya if elected.

The net result of the policy of yielding to pressures from two opposite sides was that none of the communities was satisfied with the ruling Congress Party, which lost power in the 1989 elections. Again, the major beneficiary in the situation was the BJP. The executive of the party which met at Palampur in Himachal Pradesh on June 11, 1989, resolved to make construction of the Ram temple at the site of the Babri masjid its election plank. Its president L K Advani was confident that the resolution "will translate into votes".[18]

The BJP increased its strength in the Lok Sabha from two in the elections held in November 1984 (when a martyred Indira Gandhi had stolen the thunder of the BJP's militant nationalism and had consolidated Hindu vote in favour of the Congress) to 86 in 1989. As a main prop of the minority government of V P Singh, the BJP acquired a decisive say in the affairs of the government. Its influence on Kashmir policy of the government and close understanding with Jagmohan, who was appointed governor of the state in January 1990, enabled it to make Kashmir the second major plank of its political offensive.

'Hindus under siege'

In the 80s one could discern some changes in the political and religious mind of the Hindus. The fear that they might be outnumbered on account of convertions (such as the one took place in Meenakshipuram in 1981), the alleged faster rate of growth of the Muslim population as a result of polygamy (underlined by the Shah Bano episode), and the continuing infiltration of Bangladeshi Muslims into India (as a part of a 'conspiracy'), coupled with the perceived threat to national unity and the Hindu interests by the Muslim, Sikh and Christian secessionists and terrorists (in Kashmir, Punjab and the North-East), created a siege mentality among the Hindus. The growing assertion of the Muslims within the country and Islamic resurgence in the Muslim world added to the siege consciousness.

The Vishwa Hindu Parishad, a member of the RSS family of organizations, assumed the role of defining and standardizing religious identity of the Hindus. The inferiority complex that gripped a section of the community encouraged a process of its semitisation in order to meet the perceived threat from the Semitic religions. Demolition of the Babri masjid was sought to avenge the past 'humiliations'. The agitation for Ram Janmabhoomi was launched to project a national hero Ram as the foremost incarnation of God and Ayodhya as the Mecca of the Hindus.

The developments in the Hindu and Muslim psyche in the 80s demolished many traditional bridges between the two communities. The decline of ideologies, the party system, and institutions of justice, law and order; and communalization of administrative machinery, criminalisation of politics and collapse of inter-community dialogue contributed to fresh wave of communal violence. Killings at Hashimpura, Maliana (1987) and Bhagalpur (1989) set a new record of riot toll in independent India. In the last year of the decade, there were 18 major riots taking a toll of 1,174 lives.[19]

The 90s did not start with a peaceful note. It was the year of L K Advani's rath yatra which left a trail of blood at many places. The BJP launched a frontal attack on the traditional secular parties by calling them pseudo-secularist and pseudo-nationalist, and declared itself against the 'policy of appeasement of the minorities'. Perhaps for the first time, the BJP president, Advani was frank enough to admit to the BBC on July 29, 1990 that "it would not be wrong to call the BJP a Hindu Party".[20]

But it was the issue of the Ram Janmabhoomi, spear-headed by the VHP, which gave the BJP maximum political mileage. Initially, the issue involved a legal dispute over a piece of land which should have been resolved in a judicial court. Later, the Muslim leaders offered to forego their claim over the mosque if it was established that the Babri masjid was built after destroying a Ram temple. It then became an archeological issue which should have been settled by national or international experts.

Revival of Muslim confidence

However, the successive governments managed to convert it into a Hindu-Muslim problem. They also recognized BJP-VHP combine as the sole representative of the Hindu community. This status was imposed on it when the BJP had only two members in the Lok Sabha. No other group challenged its credentials or staked its own claim to represent the community. The liberals assumed a neutral role of preaching settlement of the issue through a dialogue between the two 'parties' or through a verdict of the court.

As the party of the Hindus in the dispute, a status impliedly conceded to it by the liberals, the BJP earned political windfalls. By 1991, it emerged as the recognized opposition in parliament with 119 members and a ruling party in four Hindi speaking states, including the crucial UP.

In sharp contrast, no single group either claimed to be or was recognized as the sole representative of the Muslim community. The two committees that represented its case were just broad-based coalitions of diverse elements in the community.

The bid to out-semitise Islam, to theologise, monolithise and regiment Hinduism, which, strictly speaking, was not a religion but "a parliament of religions"[21] or a way of life-evolved over thousands of years, incorporating and assimilating a bewildering diversity of beliefs and sub-cultures-created more problems for Hindus than for Muslims. Neither the sadhus and saints, drawn from different sects and traditionally far-removed from the mainstream of the Hindu society, were able to project a unified religious vision or leadership nor the muscle power of the Bajrang Dal could impose uniformity.

While regional and ethnic cultures maintained their zealously guarded autonomy within the Hindu fold, the decision of the V P Singh government to implement Mandal Commission's recommendations regarding reservation of jobs for what are called OBCs (other backward classes) stimulated caste consciousness which acted as another brake to the movement for uniformity and homogenization of Hinduism. The conflict over the management of the Bodh Gaya temple between the neo-Buddhists (mostly dalits) and VHP indicated resurgence of urge for dalit and Buddhist identity and its clash with the forces of Hindutva.

As the BJP's Hindutva plank improved its caste Hindu base, electoral importance of Muslims became more crucial for other parties. A series of concessions were included in the non-BJP party manifestoes to win over the Muslim support. Announcement of national holiday on the birthday of the prophet of Islam, grant of the second language status to Urdu in the UP and of statutory status to the Minorities Commission, prohibition to change the status of religious places as they existed in 1947, and constitution of Rapid Action Force (RAF) to expeditiously and effectively control riots were among the steps taken within less than first two years of the 90s.

On the critical issue of Babri masjid, all non-BJP parties made a categorical commitment against its demolition. The prime minister Narasimha Rao announced it from the rampart of the Red Fort, on independence day, 1992, that the Ram temple would be constructed without demolishing the mosque. The left and the national front lodged a dogged protest in parliament, blocking its proceedings for several days, against the move of the UP government to allow construction around the disputed land till an all-party delegation was sent to Ayodhya for on the spot inquiry. Thus the Hindu- Muslim dispute changed into a dispute between secular and communal forces till it was again referred to 'the concerned parties' the VHP, as usual, representing the Hindus.

The overall impact of these developments was a perceptible revival of the confidence of the Muslim community in itself, in secular parties, and in the institutions of the state. The Muslim leaders and the Muslim press started articulating and rationalizing the interests and problems of the community not from a parochial, communal angle but, as part of the secular front, in a secular idiom. They criticized Hindu communalism, not as a threat to the community but to the national unity and national values like secularism and democracy. They insisted that they had as much right to define nationalism and national interest as the Hindus.

Meanwhile, a new Muslim middle class of both men and women-professionals, academics, writers, technicians and managers - emerged, spurred partly by the Gulf boom. With its newly acquired prestige and its modern outlook, it gave an impetus to social reforms and to the spread of education, particularly technical. A campaign against social evils, like dowry and triple divorce by the All India Muslim Personal Law Board, the conduct of Taleemi (educational) caravan, led by former AMU vice-chancellor, preaching need for modern education, through Muslim-dominated areas of UP, and the publication of papers and journals in Hindi and English are some of the illustrations of the impact of the new middle class in Muslim social life in early 90s.

India Today, which did a cover story on the subject, observed: "The Muslim community is in a state of flux and turmoil as it emerges from its isolation and insecurity into a brave new world where its concerns and aspirations are the same as everyone else's in India. Young Muslims are the engines of far-reaching change affecting attitudes and life-styles."[22]

Demolition of Masjid

Before such trends in Muslim attitude and life could crystalise, the community was rudely shaken, as it never was in independent India, by the demolition of the Babri masjid on December 6, 1992. Indeed, the whole nation felt the shock which many compared with what it felt on the assassination of Gandhi in 1948.

Babri Masjid was neither the first nor the last mosque or place of worship to be demolished since independence. But never before had a community staked its prestige on protecting a religious place. The Operation Blue Star was an assault on the holiest place of the Sikhs. But it had demonstrated the power of the Indian state. Ayodhya outrage, on the other hand, exposed how weak the Indian state could choose to be. It also demonstrated the helplessness of institutions like the Supreme Court, Parliament and the National Integration Council. All political parties including the BJP, which had pledged that the mosque would not be harmed, proved equally helpless. The communal violence that followed the demolition further showed that the state machinery could not merely feign to be helpless in protecting the Muslim minority, but also that it could be hostile to it.

The ideological forces that had attacked Gandhi may have been similar to those that attacked the Babri masjid. But the aftermath in the two cases was dissimilar. Gandhi's blood extinguished a communal conflagration. The demolition ignited a deadly conflagration. In 1948, the target of the Hindu fanatics was a Hindu. In 1992, the targeted building was projected as a symbol of Hindu humilitation at the hands of a Muslim ruler, a foreign invader.

On the positive side, however, all non-BJP parties, almost the entire media, the intellectual and moral leadership, and the community of artists, writers and academics, unequivocally condemned the Ayodhya vandalism. Even the BJP equivocated for a while with its senior leader, Atal Bihari Vajpaye expressed his anguish, sorrow and dissent more explicitly. Many sensitive Hindus felt alarmed at the ugly manifestation of Hindu extremism which was seeking to monolithise, lumpenise and degenerate Hinduism, and was threatening the very basis of the republic, its secular character, the sanctity of the Constitution, judiciary and other democratic institutions, and the basic values of the Indian civilization.

In fact, the sharp division between the RSS Hindus and the non-RSS Hindus-the sharpest ever schism in the community - undermined the Hindu-Muslim divide. The offensive against the Sangh parivar by the secular parties tended to bring the Muslim masses closer to the mainstream. They were, however, disillusioned with the established Musilm leaders, who were spearheading the cause of the Babri Masjid, for their failure to protect it and articulate their anger into an effective and concrete line of action after its demolition. The two Babri masjid committees thought it prudent to leave the matter to the more broad-based Muslim Personal Law Board, formed at the time of the Shah Bano case and led by a prestigious personality like Ali Mian.

Revival of Liberal Muslims

Inspired by the role of the secular liberal Hindus and encouraged by the decline in the prestige of the hitherto dominant Muslim leadership, liberal Muslims, too, came out of their hibernation and asserted their right to represent the community. The Muslim intelligentsia, representing Muslim academicians, professionals and journalists, which first came together in Delhi on January 24, 1993, challenged the memorandum of the Muslim Personal Law Board to the prime minister rejecting his package on the issue of the Babri masjid and alleged that it "represents the opinion of a section of Ulama and discredited politicians".[23] The meet urged the government to try to evolve a consensus on the issue by eliciting opinion from a wide section of both Hindus and Muslims, instead of negotiating only with religious leaders.

Another group of Muslim film personalities and journalists expressed "pain and dismay" at the "rigid, unrealistic and confrontationist stand" of the Board on the temple-mosque dispute and said, "the Board did not represent the views of the entire community."[24]

Expressing the newly acquired confidence by Muslim liberals, JS Bandukwala exclaimed: "An air of liberalism is sweeping the Muslim community. Suddenly the Muslim liberal is the man of the hour. Gone are the days when such views were anathema and their bearers branded as Kaffirs. The shift in Muslim opinion may be the most important consequence of the Babri masjid demolition." He asked Hindus to give Muslim liberals a chance. The BJP leaders like Atal Bihari Vajpayee welcomed the new Muslim mood. There was also an informal dialogue between them and some Muslim intellectuals at BJP sponsored seminars and iftar parties. How it came to power at the Centre through a broad based coalition, including non-communal and non-Hindutva parties is discussed elsewhere in detail.

A similar practice of coalition making by the Congress ensured its return to power in 2004. Hindutva wave was stemmed in the UP and Bihar by an alliance of OBC and Muslims. An outstanding instance of marginalisation of the BJP in 2007 election was the way BSP leader Mayawati was able to work out a coalition of castes led by a Dalit. That way even casteism has been made to play a positive role in stregthening a secular, democratic and egalitarian system.

Notes

1. *Rooh-I-Makateeb Iqbal,* Iqbal Academy, Lahore, p. 638.
2. Moin Shakir, *Muslims in Free India.*
3. Gopal Krishna in *Muslim Communities of South Asia,* edited by TN Madan, Vikas, p. 154.
4. Quoted by M A Karandikar, *Islam in Tradition to Modemity,* Orient Longman, 1968.
5. Quoted by C P Bhambri, *Financial Express,* May 24, 1992.
6. K L Gauba, *Passive Voices,* Sterling, 1973, p. 282.
7. *The Times of India,* August 12,1965.
8. B P L Bedi, *India, Indian Muslims and Pakistan,* New Delhi, 1965.
9. Quoted in *Radiance,* February 18-24, 1990.
10. Editorial in *Radiance,* January 28- February 3, 1990.
11. *The Times of India,* April 28, 1987.
12. W C Smith, Islam in Modem History, Princeton University Press, 1957, p. 266-67 13. *Religion, Law and State in India,* Free Press, New York, 1968.
14. *Dawat,* Delhi, November 7,1967.
15. N S Saxena, *The Times o/India,* January 4,1988.
16. Referring to the repeated but unimplemented assurance of the) RSS leaders to include non- Hindus- Muslims, Christians; etc-in it, J P lamented, “its continuing like this for the last four years. After a;; there is a limit to every thing”, *Dinman Weekly,* April 8-14, 1979.

17. Jalalul Haq, *Nation and Nation-worship in India,* Genuine publications, Delhi, 1992, p. 89.
18. *The Hindustan Times,* June 12, 1989.
19. Written reply of the union minister of state for home affairs M M Jacob in the Rajya Sabhaon July 17,1991.
20. *Organiser,* August 5, 1990.
21. Charles Elliot, *Hinduism and Buddhism,* Vol. 1, p. XXXIV.
22. October 31, 1992.
23. *The Times of India,* April 9, 1993.
24. *Ibid,* April 10, 1993.
25. *The Times of India,* February 16, 1993.
26. The Telegraph, June 20, 1992.

(Economic & Political Weekly, Vol. XXVIII. No. 40, October 2, 1993)

3

Understanding Indian Muslims

During the America led war against global terrorism, a controversy arose on the attitude of Indian Muslims. Those who did not support fundamentalism, communalism, puritanism and militant Islam and hence are not disloyal to the country were asked to speak out and be counted. The liberal Muslims protested that media noticed only the extremist view point and ignored them who represented the silent majority.

The fact however, cannot be denied that Muslims all over the world have been affected by a sort of anti-America wave, in varying degrees, notwithstanding stand of their respective governments and their internal contradictions. There are a number of reasons for this, including post modem communication revolution which has drastically reduced distances between members of a community and sharpened their urge for identity. Clash of civilizations thesis and America's perceived anti-Muslim policies further consolidated the current Muslim mood. Nobody is more conscious of it than leaders of the anti-terrorism coalition. Extensive diplomatic efforts, tours of the Muslim countries and Iftar parties to neutralise Muslim hostility bear that out.

India had obvious advantages in playing its role in the emerging international situation. Not only its large Muslim population, which had played a leading role in the constructive evolution of Islamic thought, but also its traditional relations with Muslim countries as a leader of the non-aligned block of which most of them were members, were its unique assets.

Far from using our external and internal assets to evolve a consensus on possible attitude towards American policies and global terrorism, this very issue was sought to be used as a new loyalty test for the Muslims of India by a section of our countrymen. Take the case of Shahi Imam, for instance. Granted that Islam does not recognise Shahi or any other special status for any Imam. Granted that his views are obscurantist and parochial and his expression is intemperate. But how do these characteristics qualify him to be disloyal to the country?

The Imam had also condemned General Parvez Musharraf for betraying Islam whom the Muslims of Pakistan would teach a lesson. He also condemned jehad in Kashmir as anti-Islam. Anti-Pakistanism and Indian sovereignty over Kashmir have been prescribed as a test of patriotism for Muslims by the nationalist Hindus. Why then Imam was branded anti-national and demands were made for his arrest on the charge of sedition? Why did the police pounce upon Muslim youth in Malegaon and tore off the posters which urged boycott of products of American companies? When Muslims of Kashmir demonstrated against American bombing of Afghanistan, without raising pro-Pak or anti-India slogans, why did Indian authorities feel scared?

The question is not whether these manifestations of the Muslims view point represent majority or minority of the community and whether they are right or wrong. The real question relates to the concept of Indian nationalism and to know which one of the view points cited above defies it.

Again, the widely held presumption that Muslims are more easily swayed by the appeal of religion needs to be examined more closely. In this context a comparison between the personalities of Maulana Azad and MA Jinnah has already been quoted in the preceding pages. While the former claimed that the Quran was the sole source of his knowledge, the latter was completely ignorant of it. Azad with his humanitarian and cosmopolitan interpretation of the Quran led the Ulama almost as a class, to become an ally of Indian nationalism led by Gandhi. Jinnah, steeped in western culture, was for all practical purposes a non-practicing Muslim. He defied many strict Islamic injunctions in his personal life.

The moral of pre-partition clash between the two approaches was clear viz Jinnah's concerns for Muslim identity and its mundane political and economic interests expressed in non-religious language triumphed over religious appeal of Islamic scholars and Ulama led by Azad.

Indian Ulama have no doubt made a seminal and original contribution to the growth of Islamic thought. But historically their role in shaping Muslim mind and spread of Islam has been far less than that of the Sufis and the politicised establishment of Muslim Kings, none of them practiced Islamic codes being preached by modem fundamentalists. Sufis freely borrowed local customs and culture and preached more through music, poetry and humane conduct than through quotations from scriptures and prescribing rigid religious code of conduct. Most of the Kings were hedonists and indulged in wine, women and all good things of life. They patronised dance, music and painting, some of which are prohibited by orthodox Islam.

If Urdu language, to which Muslims, in North India are attached next to their religion, is any guide of Muslims culture, the heterodox tradition of Indian Muslims borders heresy. The words like Kaffir and Sannam (idol) the main targets of radical Islam are used in Urdu poetry as synonym with beloved. Maikada (bar) and Butkada (house of idols) take precedence over places of worship. Wine, women and physical beauty are the most celebrated subjects of its poetry.

Nowhere else did Islam confront as ancient a civilization, as speculative and pluralistic philosophical thought, and as non-combative but resilient a faith as in India. Similarly, no other Muslim community has had as long and direct exposure to rationalism, modern knowledge and institutions, of the west. Thus as observed by India's most respected Islamic scholar Sayeed Abul Hasan Ali Nadvi, "The Indian Muslims occupy a place of distinction in the Islamic world by virtue of their various intellectual and moral qualities and in some respect they are superior to all other Muslim communities. They are capable of lending help and guidance to free and independent Muslim countries in many fields of intellectual and literary endeavour.

If, in spite of these facts, some Muslims of India today betray tendencies towards any kind of fundamentalist, puritan and militant Islam, it is for the whole nation to find out its reasons and remedies and not for the Muslims alone. In any case it should not be easy to provoke or tempt a community so proud of its Indianness to develop extra-territorial loyalties.

The controversy over interpretations of the verses of the Quran between the 'liberals" and the "fundamentalists" is hardly much relevant in this context. A community's heritage is much more than a set of theological beliefs of the scriptures to which it owes allegiance. To some extent culture is autonomous of and precedes scriptures. Cultural heritage and political aspirations of a community are as much a factor in influencing its behaviour as its theological beliefs.

While religious scholars may continue their search in discovering further evidence for what Maulana Azad had, on the basis of his interpretation of Quran, had established viz "essential unity of all faiths," it is equally important to understand cultural heritage of Indian Muslims which they share at national and to a greater extent at regional level with non-Muslims.

Politically nothing hurts them more than special loyalty tests that are being prescribed for them. Their transnational links are a reality. But they can become a national asset if they are helped to become a self-confident and secure nationals of the country. The contribution of Indian Ulama, Sufis, Muslim poets and artists is so rich that no other Muslim community of the world can inspire or win over the loyalty of Indian Muslims. They have a right to be inheritors of a 5000 year old civilisation and citizens of a genuinely functioning democratic and plural country.

The debate between liberals and non-liberals between Hindus and Muslims may continue. But it would generate more light than mere heat if everybody is able to proclaim a proud inheritor of the great composite heritage of India.

(*The Hindu,* December 17, 2001)

4

Autonomy and Participation Dimensions of Indian Muslim Identity

Broadly, Muslims of India manifest their urge of identity at three levels: Pan-Islamic, Subcontinental, and National. They also invariably possess non-religious identities, like belonging to a region, class, party; profession, and so on. These identities (mostly shared with other religious communities) are as much a part of objective reality as Muslim identity.

With the collapse of the Khilafat and the rise of sovereign Muslim states whose interests are not always the same, pan-Islamism has virtually exhausted its capacity to rally Muslims of the world under a single political system. On occasions and issues-such as that of Israel or Iraq - Muslim sentiment the world over might tend to react in a similar manner. Oil power of some Muslim countries might also provide an economic viability to such common reactions. But they cannot completely supplant national identities of Muslims or lead to an effective supra-national authority with a single political centre.

In any case, whatever be the degree of revival of this Pan-Islamic sentiment, Muslims in India need not always be an embarrassment or liability for the country. For Pan-Islamism had had provided additional friendly bond between India and the Muslim countries of the world. Gandhi and ardent nationalist Muslims like Abdul Kalam Azad and MA Ansari, in fact, treated Pan-Islamism as a definite ally of Indian nationalism in its struggle for independence. They championed the cause of Khilafat, the last experiment of a pan-Islamic state. till it faced a revolt in Turkey, the rulers of which had claimed that right.

Subcontinental Muslim Identity

While the Pan-Islamic idea has romantic and abstract characteristics, subcontinental Muslim identity has a deeper emotional, cultural, racial and historical basis. Pakistan, claimed to be a homeland of the Muslims of undivided India, was demanded more intensely by those who now form part of the present India. It is the subcontinental Muslim community which "today leads the Muslims of the world in their zeal and practical behaviour for the spread of their faith."[1]

However, their overzealous urge for political identity and autonomy to the extent of nationhood, is now universally acknowledged to have been not in their own best interests. According to the veteran Muslim League leader, Khaliq-uz-Zaman, "the two nations theory proved positively injurious to the Muslims in India, and on a long view basis for Muslims everywhere."[2]

Extending the stern logic of the two nations theory, Jamaat-e-Islami leader Maulana Maudoodi, who, too, migrated to Pakistan, gave the following advice to his followers left behind in India: "We should try to create on a large scale public opinion among the Muslims that they should, as a community, have nothing to do with the government and its administration and should assure Hindu nationalism by their attitude that there is no other political nationality in the field to fight against it." While pleading for an Islamic state for Pakistan, he found nothing wrong in the formation of Hindu Raj in India. Advising Muslims to "change their attitude completely", Jammat-e-Islami Hind considered it "terribly suicidal" for "Muslims to strive for some communal rights."[3]

IH Qureshi was so pessimistic as to predict that "In a hundred years, perhaps in a shorter time, the Muslim people may cease to exist in" India.[4]

Potentialities of Indian Islam

In refreshing contrast to these prophets of doom, W.C. Smith struck a startlingly optimistic note about the future of Islam in India in as early as 1957. Without quite anticipating later events such as the disintegration of Pakistan in 1971, he believed that "Islam in India would emerge as more progressive, dynamic, liberal and creative than Pakistani Islam."[5] This belief is not entirely unfounded. For it is the Muslims of India who alone have inherited the continuity of history, tradition, and culture of the subcontinent; whereas Pakistan and Bangladesh have only borrowed them from India. Important Islamic institutions - like Aligarh, Deoband, and Jamia and prestigious symbols of what is called Muslim glory like the Red Fort and the Taj Mahal - have remained in India. The real home of Urdu - the official language of Pakistan - is also here. Even the essence of the concept of Islam dominant in the other two countries was evolved in the Indian part of the subcontinent, by Chishti order to Ulama of Deoband and other institutions of Islamic learning, and its secular practices were shaped by the policies of the imperial Muslim rulers of Delhi.

The basic fact, that a section of Muslims of India and their tradition and culture were incorporated by Pakistan, and to a lesser extent by Bangladesh - and not the other way round - has already asserted itself.

Pak-Indians

In this context the significant role of Pak-Indians, the term now commonly used for Urdu-speaking emigrants from India to Pakistan has been discussed in Chapter 6.

Geopolitical Centre

Indian Muslims no doubt cherish subcontinental affinities. But these neither amount to any political allegiance to a foreign land, nor imply that they must necessarily look across the border for emotional, moral and intellectual support in a one-way traffic. The reverse trend - of a bigger traffic - has already been noticed.

Moreover, with two-thirds of the population of the Muslims of the subcontinent being out of Pakistan, Islamabad is no more in a position to remain the centre of their inspiration. Geohistorically, Delhi is now better placed for that role.

The split of Pakistan itself was not merely a physical biow to it but also to its ideology. It demonstrated that, even for the Muslims of the subcontinent - and of Pakistan — , language and culture can have as powerful an appeal as religion. Moreover, the two resultant nations which are striving to function on the basis of Islamic thought have yet not been able to evolve a stable and appropriate form of it - or a theory of government in consonance with it - to meet the demands of a modem state. Even the residual Pakistani nation seems to be groping for a viable ideology, identity, and, in fact, its very raison d'etre. Its failure, to meet the urges of multi-cultural identities like Bloachis, Pushtoons, Muhajirs and Sindhis and develop a functioning and stable polity, has also undermined its position and claim as a source of inspiration for the Muslims of the subcontinent.

Contest for Pakistan's Soul

Pakistan's identity is not so much threatened by its traditional enemy, India, as by the fraternal embraces of its two oil giant neighbours-Saudi Arabia and Iran. "Indeed the contest over Pakistan's soul is one of the bitterest differences between the two".[6] Having lived on a borrowed ideology (Indian Islam), a borrowed history (Indo Islamic), a borrowed language (Urdu), and a borrowed leadership (Jinnah, Liaqat, Bhutto and Musharraf), Pakistan can snap its bonds with India only at its peril -notwithstanding the appeal of the home of Islam (Arabia) and cultural home of upper-class Pakistanis (Iran). In fact, it would be in Pakistan's interest to use Indian influence on it to maintain a balance of external influences. And it would be in India's interests to guarantee Pakistan's viability.

Urdu is unlikely to be replaced by Persian or Arabic, whatever be their cultural or religious sanctity. Punjabi and Sindhi are fast aspiring to take a part of its place. What is more likely to happen - and is in the real interest of the country - is that the people of Pakistan would seek roots in their own soil and historical continuity with their own past, pre-dating Islam. Local warriors and rulers - Muslim and non-Muslim - who resisted outside Muslim invasions and the authority of Muslim kingdoms of Delhi are already becoming their new heroes. Books like "5000 years of Pakistan" and "the Indus Saga"[7], are adding further to the list of questions about the country's history, tradition, identity, and continuity - which contradict the objectives for which Pakistan, was originally conceived and founded.

To the extent that such regional culture and regional patriotism grow, the concept of Muslim solidarity and what is called the 'Ideology of Pakistan' will have to be revised and diluted. In that case, emotional and cultural bonds of Pak-Indians with the land of their origin would be revived and strengthened. As Indian polity is based on a recognition of regional cultures, the struggle of Muslims of Pakistan for similar recognition of their well-defined cultural identities and for their political and constitutional autonomy is bound to look to India for inspiration and precedence. Already, the Pashtoon movement, the Bloach rebellion, Sindhi patriotism, and the campaign of Pak-Indians, are being dubbed pro-India, even though these have received no active help from India. Furthermore, an account of India's geopolitical importance, its size and past, the relatively better performance of its political and administrative institutions, its democratic system, its superior material, technological, and military strength, India is becoming an attractive model for the intelligentsia of Pakistan and Bangladesh. In their struggle for the restoration of civil liberties, they tend to look to India for moral support.

Muslims and Indian Nationalism

As Muslims in India are seeking a role within a universe of non-Muslim majority - which is exactly what Muslims are doing in the world as a whole - India has become a unique laboratory for the future role of the world Muslim community. Besides experimenting with how to share power with a non-Muslim majority, Muslims in a part of India (Kashmir) are also experimenting with how to share power with a non-Muslim minority. Both experiments have far-reaching significance not only for India but also for the future of Islam. For, it has been said that Muslims elsewhere and in the past have, generatly speaking, either ruled or have been ruled. There are very few precendents of their having shared power.

As Indonesia never mattered much in Muslim history, and as (judging by the foregoing discussion) Pakistan seems to be losing the race to India both as a nation state and in its contribution to Islam, Smith might not have been entirely wrong in suggesting that the potentialities of Islam in India are comparable only to those it has in the Arab world. And even Arab nation states are far from a harmonious region and each one of them is vastly outnumbered by the Muslims of India.

But how wide is the gap between the promise that Islam in India holds and the reality that Muslims in India represent? In other words, "why, in spite of all legal rights, Indian Muslims continue to be backward" miserable, and estranged?"[8]

While the compatibility of the transnational aspects of the identity of Muslims of India - Pan-Islamic as well as subcontinental - with the national interest is established by the foregoing analysis, the terms between their identity at national level and Indian nationalism do not seem to have been clearly settled. The debate on the subject ranges from pleas for completely eliminating all communal identities to reorganization of Indian polity as a federation of religious communities.

Harman supports the former plea. In order to "end the plight of Muslims in India", he advises them to merge their identity into the main-stream" by adopting Hindu names, surnames and castes."[9]

The advice is too impractical to merit any serious discussion. It is neither possible nor even desirable to eliminate all intermediate identities and loyalties that do exist between the individual and the nation. Uniformity, in fact, is the shortest route to disunity. In a country of India's vastness, complexity and diversity, an intense and exclusive national loyalty which does not take cognizance of sub-national identities is likely to arouse different responses among different sections of the nation which would have disrupting and disintegrating potentialities.

Moreover, there is hardly any unanimity in the country on a clear concept and full content of Indian nationalism. In any case, the emotional appeal of nationalism does not remain at a constant pitch for ever. Many sectional sentiments, which get suppressed at time of external threats, natural calamities and outstanding achievements, assert themselves in normal times; and many sentiments dormant in normal times are aroused on some particular occasions.

The intensity of Muslim identification with nationalist sentiments can thus vary with time and issue. The variation is not always along communal lines. The emotional reaction to the emergence of Bangladesh was, for instance, far more intense in West Bengal than elsewhere in the country. The emotional involvement of the people in issues, such as Tibet, Kashmir, Vietnam and Czechoslovakia, was also not uniform among all regions and all parties of India. Likewise, even Indian history would appear different if viewed from the perspective of different regions or from the standpoint of different ideologies. However, in pre-Independent India the dominant Muslim sentiment was not only out of step with Indian nationalism but also drifted away from it in another direction. Historically, Muslim communalism was a reaction to the concept of Indian nationalism which was shaped by Hindu religious personalities from Aurobindo to Gandhi. Jinnah reacted against Gandhi, who mattered, and not against Savarkar.Though he found direct support for his two nations theory from Savarkar who had said in 1937: " There are two nations in the main, the Hindu and Muslim in India."[10] Both thus rejected Gandhi's idea of one nation.

Muslims of India have resisted 'Indianisation' of various brands - the crude as well as the sophisticated - beyond a degree where their distinct entity is threatened.

Harman is surprised that Indian Muslims do not own the Indian heritage which they should, as good nationalists. After all, Muslims of other countries do take pride in their pre-Islamic past. Pre-Islamic epics, like *Sikandaranama* and *Shahnama*, are part of the cultural heritage of Iran. Indeed, these also form a part of folklore of many Muslim homes in India. But why do they not own Ramayana and Mahabharata, which are a vital ingredient of the culture of a Muslim country such as Indonesia, it is asked.

Apart from the minority character and historical background of Muslim Indians, it is the peculiar character of Hinduism which influences their attitude. More than a creed or a set of practices, Hinduism is a geographical and racial entity. It is confined to Indians or people of Indian origin. For most Hindus, as Aurobindo put it, "nationalism is religion." Indian history merges into Hindu religion so that ancient heroes, epics and literature have a religious character.

Dilemma of Muslim Indian

The dilemma of a Muslim Indian is that in his journey back to his own history - history of his own country - he slips into a domain that also belongs to another religion. Hinduism meets Islam not as just another creed but as a representative of the ancient and native heritage of the nation. It is the assimilative and integrationist character of Hinduism - and not its communal brand - that seems to threaten the Muslim identity.

However, a rigid concept of Indian nationalism and heritage is not shared by many Hindu cultural groups and intellectuals as well. In a Tamil version of Ramayana, for instance, the character of Rama and Ravana could be portrayed quite differently from what they are in the versions of Valmiki or Tulsidas.

No sensible Muslim would, on the other hand, show such disrespect to Rama and Krishna. Some are, in fact, inclined to include them among the list of prophets, who according to the

Koran, appeared among all communities of the world in all ages and are worthy of respect as prophets of Islam. Even many Hindus, including Swami Dayanand, treat them only as great men and not as incarnations of God.

Theological controversies may not, therefore, be so insurmountable and beyond the ingenuity of Muslim scholars of India to tackle. In fact, Muslims theologists have, on the whole, made a positive contribution to the evolution of the concept of composite Indian nationalism.

Secondly Indian nationalism was challenged not so much by theologists as by that section of Muslim leadership which was more concerned with the secular problems of the community - its education, employment opportunities, representation in administration and political institutions like legislature and share in political power - than with Islamic theories. It is also worth noting that theological interpretations alone have never been the decisive factor in the conduct of Muslims of India. "The necessity of *ijtihad* - innovation in Islamic thought - was therefore emphasised by Sir Syed as well as by Iqbal". They also incurred wrath of Ulama who issued fatwas against both of them for their alleged heresies.

Whether the political ideas of Syed Ahmed, Iqbal and Jinnah served the real interests of Muslims is beside the point. But these modernized leaders certainly represented the urges and aspirations of Muslims better than the Ulama. Modernisation, it would seem, sharpened consciousness of a distinct Muslim identity which Islamic thought and Muslim tradition had given it.

Modernisation and Muslim Identity

The larger number of pilgrims to Haj and Islamic shrines and the increase in number and circulation of Urdu papers (the most widely read language by Muslims) would bear out the fact that Muslim consciousness is growing with the pace of modernization.

The Muslim community which has successfully resisted assimilative attractions of Hinduism can, even in the event of sharpening of ethnic cleavages as a result of modernisation, confidently aspire to preserve its identity. The potential threats to national integration from this identity, too, have been reduced now. In fact, the Muslim community has on many occasions demonstrated its identification with the national interest. Indeed, a multiplicity of identities and a pluralistic system are considered basic attributes of democracy and a school of thought among the Hindus, which is keen to maintain their identity and unity, in fact concedes to Muslims a more explicit entity.

The forms and manifestations of Muslims identity or identities and the degree of its autonomy, therefore, may not be viewed exclusively in terms of Hindu-Muslim relations. For, as has been pointed out earlier, Hindu chauvinists and Muslim chauvinists are likely to agree more with each other than with liberals of other communities on the nature of communal identities.

Only one set of implications of modernization has been discussed above. While modernisation would tend to increase awareness of ethnic identities, the needs and urges of a modern man are becoming too complex to be satisfied by a single identity. Multiplicity of identities to which an individual now inevitably belongs acts as a check on exclusiveness and parochialism of particular identities and prevents them from becoming rivals to national entity.

In discussing the question of Muslim identity, it must be noted that, like all other identities based on class, caste, culture, region and ideology, it is not exclusive and monolithic. A Muslim may derive inspiration from his faith, owe allegiance to common symbols of the community, faithfully follow its rituals and manifest his identity in various fields of life. But he cannot help identifying himself with different sets of people belonging to other faiths in his social, cultural, professional and to some extent even in political life for full growth of his personality. Thus 'Muslim identity' needs to be differentiated from and supplemented by 'Identities of Muslims' - which they inevitably share with others and which satisfy their multiple urges as full-fledged human beings.

Reconciliation of Muslims

In this context, regional identity, the fourth level of identities in the vertical order that we have been discussing - after international (Pan-Islamic), subcontinental, and national - is of crucial importance for the Musilm community. It is at this level that the community can find roots in the soil and get integrated with other communities more harmoniously. As regional identities, regional cultures, regional histories and regional heroes are generaliy not much coloured by standarised Hinduism, Muslims tend to own their pre-Islamic heritage at the regional level more readily than they do it at the national level. In fact, in each region of the country, there are saints, reformers, and warriors who symbolize its common and composite heritage and inspire emotional allegiance of all its communities. But such symbols are fewer at the national level. While many Muslim faquirs and pirs are revered by non-Muslims at local levels, Krishna is integrated into Muslim consciousness at folk level in Braj and Mewat areas but not elsewhere.

Even Chhatrapati Shivaji and Maharana Pratap, who are projected as symbols of Hindu revivalism at the national level for having struggled against the so-called foreign Muslim rule, were essentially regional heroes who endeavoured to protect the autonomy and rights of Marathwar and Mewar, respectively, against the then central national authority - as did many regional Muslim rulers at that time. Similarly, Guru Nanak and Baba Farid represent the common spiritual heritage of Hindus, Muslims and Sikhs of Punjab, on both sides of the international border. Tagore and Nazar-ul-Islam also represent the indivisible common cultural heritage of not only Hindus and Muslims but also of India and Bangladesh. Regionalisation is thus undoubtedly the single greatest integrating force between various communities and, in the case of Punjab and Bengal, between nations of the subcontinent.

It is no accident that Kashmiri and Pushtoon Muslims, who were intensely proud of their respective regional cultures, became the main bulwark against the communal movement of the Muslim League sweeping over the rest of the subcontinent. The process of regionalisation (hence of secularization) of Muslims has been more pronounced where they constituted a majority, where their Muslim identity had been ensured. Historically, also the peripheral regions of the subcontinent, including Muslim majority areas like Kashmir, Frontier, and Bengal, have regarded imperial rulers of Delhi like the Mughals as aggressors and have manifested deeper regional consciousness. But the process is unmistakably extending to Muslims of other areas as well. The arguments used earlier to prove a positive correlation between modernization and communal consciousness apply with equal force to that between modernization and regional consciousness.

But what would be the correlation between regional and communal consciousness? Both are likely to be sharpened as a consequence of modernization, coexisting with and to some extent also balancing each other. Bangladesh would illustrate the point. Muslim Bengal asserted its Muslim personality in 1947 against its co-linguistic Hindu neighbours. Twenty four years later, it asserted its regional personality also, though a revolt against its co-religionist West Pakistanis. But 1971 did not contradict 1947; it only supplemented 1947. Emergence of Bangladesh, above all, demonstrated that a Bengali Muslim was a Bengali as well as a Muslims. In the case of Kashmir also, Kashmir asserted its regional personality in 1947 against the threat from its co-religionist neighbours in Pakistan. But later events caused its emotional alienation from the rest of India, till it recovered from its alienation through the accord of 1975. (This balance was again disturbed fifteen years latter due to other factors) Kashmiri Muslims have throughout demonstrated that they are Kashmiris as well as Muslims.

Regional-cultural-linguistic urges are thus as vital, for Muslims as for any other community. In fact, the sense of 'identities of Muslims' - as distinct from 'Muslim identity' - would remain incomplete if these urges are not satisfied.

Though region, culture, and language, generally form an integral whole, the case of Urdu is somewhat special. Notwithstanding its secular and composite heritage, it has admittedly become a symbol of north Indian Muslim aspirations. But its role in proving a common linguistic identity to all Muslims is severely limited. It cannot replace, for instance, Kashmiri, Bengali, Malaylam, or Tamil, without culturally improvising Muslims belonging to the respective regions and distorting their integral personality.

In reality, it is the Urdu-speaking Muslim community which is most rootless and alienated and which is suffering from a crisis of identity most acutely. One reason is that it lacks a regional identity. Second, is that it lives in the heartland of Indian nationalism which, on account of its conceptual inadequacy and imprecision, does not satisfy the urges of all the communities alike. That explains why the idea of a separate Muslim homeland had its staunchest and largest support in this area.

Perhaps a new state around Delhi - which would include the Urdu speaking belt and the main centers of Islamic learning and Muslim culture of India - might satisfy some of the psychological and sociological needs of the community. Urdu can also claim and receive more intensive encouragement in this area rather than the thinly spread patronage all over the country that it is receiving today. Far from being a Muslim state it would still be of a composite character in which Muslims would remain a small minority. But a vital segment of India's Muslim aspirations would be satisfied and reconciled with those of the majority community and get a linguistic-cultural-regional sense of belonging.

Horizontal Identities

Apart from vertical levels of identities of Muslims - shared and exclusive - there are various spheres at horizontal level where their personality seeks adequate expression. The form and extent of expression would obviously vary in each sphere.

What possible role can Muslims aspire for in, say, cultural, economic and political fields?

Culture - literature, music, and art - has undoubtedly, and universally, been influenced and inspired by religion. But so has it been by numerous other factors, such as race, region, language, history, ideology, aesthetic and creative urge, and so on. The Muslims have made their mark in non-religious forms of, say, music, art and films also.

The process of regionalisation of Muslims, discussed earlier, would naturally integrate them closer to their respective regional cultures. It is, however, conceivable that, within each regional culture, there might be some symptoms of a sort of a Muslim subculture. Or to put it in another way, we could say that besides belonging to a Muslim identity, its members also share a cultured sub-entity with non-Muslims.

Similarly, social life cannot be too compartmentalized on the basis of religious affinities. Clubs, restaurants, sports and recreation, cannot and should not be segregated beyond a limit - the limit confined mainly to religious rituals and festivals.

The role of economic factors in inter-communal relations is relevant in some cases where a particular economic activity is confined to a community. But the role of class is highly exaggerated. Class and communal identities do overlap to some extent in some cases. There might also be certain economic disadvantages on account of membership of a community. In such cases economic causes act as catalytic agents and rationalisers of communal tensions. In general, common consciousness grows, in spite of and not because of, class consciousness. Communal riots in industrial towns like Jamshedpur, Rourkela and Ranchi also demonstrated that modernization, in certain circumstances, breeds communalism faster than class consciousness. However, if communal tension destroyed class solidarity in these areas, class consciousness is also known to have undermined communal identities elsewhere. Thus class and communal identities clash more often than not. After all the richest businessman of the country happens to be a Muslim.

In any case, no class system can be visualized which can be organized on the basis of religious communities. Whatever be the strength of communal sentiments, they can never completely supplant class divisions in the economic sector. How can trade unions and associations of employers be persuaded to dissolve themselves to make room for communal identities? Thus, in the economic field, Musilm can satisfy their urge for an identity by sharing it with non-Muslims, unless class and communal identities are co-terminus.

Role of Communal Parties

The real problem, however, has centred round the political role of Muslims as a community. In fact, the standard definition of communalism - is an organization of political parties exclusively on the basis of religious affiliations. If such parties are not to become a mere nuisance and a source of tensions, but are to play a meaningful role, the national polity will have to be reorganized as a federation of communities with constitutional provisions for separate electorate or proportional representation and coalition governments.

Such a model was tried in Lebanon. In Netherlands, Protestants, Catholics and Humanists share administrative authority on a similar pattern. Nearer home, Kerala has had the longest history of a coalition government. The Akali Dal was a dominant partner in Punjab government and also shared power with BJP at the Centre.

Certain limitations of these experiments must be kept in view while trying to extend them to other states of India and at the national level. The Lebanon model was, for instance, far from stabilized, and Netherlands is too small and homogenous a nation to have much lessons for India.

Among Indian models, Kerala's success is for two reasons. First, its peculiar history of caste and community identities and their inter-relations; secondly, the composition of its Muslim population which is numerous enough in some pockets to enable an exclusive Muslim party to return its candidates to the legislature on its own strength. The other Indian model (Punjab) also rests on the fact that communal distribution of population can ensure quite a few seats to an exclusively Sikh party. But, by 2007 assembly election Akali Dal had learnt the advantage of a Punjabi party over being a purely Sikh party. It gave party tickets to many Hindus to contest the election.

It is often propounded that, if Muslims maintain their political solidarity while Hindus remain divided, by ideologies, regions and castes, the former will be able to get their candidates elected in large enough number to hold the balance of Indian politics.

Hindus may be more caste-ridden than Muslims (only comparatively). But Muslims community can be immunized from ideological and regional pulls only if its emotional fervour can be maintained at a sufficiently high pitch. But that would inevitably cause a backlash in the majority community which might drown its ideological, regional and caste differences. The resultant communal polarization and tension would neither be in the interest of the Muslims nor of the country.

As India is already a federation of geographical cum cultural identities which are themselves a close rival of identities based on religious, communities, the former cannot be eliminated to make an exclusive room for the latter. Likewise ideological parties, undermine political solidarity of religious communities. Further, cultural and ideological identities meet vital emotional and intellectual needs of the members of a community. Their mental growth would suffer if they succeed in alienating themselves from these identities and in aligning exclusively with a unidimensional political identity of their community.

Religion might inspire politics. But if loyalty to a political party becomes a pre-condition for maintaining the identity of Muslims it is sure to be disrupted unless they agree to a measure of regimentation and conformism. As nothing is more vital for the interest of a minority than a democratic system, the best way of ensuring Muslim identity is to avoid giving it a political form.

Leaving aside the reaction on other communities and the considerations of national interest, a Muslim political identity is, therefore, likely to be counter-productive from the standpoint of Muslims themselves. As a matter of fact, supporters of an exclusive Hindu political party are far less averse to a similar party of Muslims than those who believe in a composite party.

However, if there are political issues which affect emotions and interests of Muslims as Muslims, their leaders, irrespective of their party affiliations, should not feel inhibited in meeting and discussing them and, if need be resorting to appropriate form of political action. But in that case also, co-operation and consultation with sympathetic leaders of other communities would be more useful and effective than any activity at communal level.

Further, short of a separate political organization for each community, other conventions and arrangements have to be devised to ensure an equitable share in political power to all communities. In this sense, secular politics must not fail to take cognizance of specific issues pertaining to religious communities, in particular minorities through appropriate institutions like the Minorities Commission.

In practice every political party which is a contender for power has got to take cognizance of the reality of communal identities. Community is, in reality, a sub-identity of every party, in other words, Muslim identity is split into political sub-identities, which Muslims share with non-Muslims.

In sum, in a complex polity like India, Muslims must belong to a multiplicity of identities, at vertical and horizontal levels, exclusive as well as in partnership with others, in order to maintain their identity and play an effective and constructive role, in peace with other communities of India, as also to satisfy their own modern multiple urges.

As followers of a great religion and citizens of a great country, Muslims of India are indeed faced with a great challenge and a great opportunity.

Notes:

1. Murray T Titus, *"Islam in India and Pakistan"*.
2. Khaliq-us-Zaman, "Pathways to Pakistan", Longman, Lahore, 1961.
3. Quoted in the official organ of the Jamat-e-Islami Hind, the *Radiance*, December 17, 1969.
4. IH Qureshi, Muslims World, XLIV, quoted by Moin Shakir in "Muslims in Free India".
5. WC Smith, "Islam in Modern History", Princeton University Press, 1957.
6. *Pakistan Economist*, April 1978.
7. Authored by Robert Eric Motimer Wheebr and Aitzaz Ahsan resectively.
8. S Harman, "Plight of Muslims in India."
9. *Ibid.*
10. K.L.Gauba, "Consequences of Pakistan" quoted by Moin Shakir, "khilafat to Partition".

(*Economic & Political Weekly.* Vol. XIII, No. 40, October 7, 1978)

5

Ethnic Dimension of Subcontinental Muslims

The ethnic riot in Karachi in December 1986 - the worst of its kind since the birth of the Islamic Republic of Pakistan - the Baloach and Pushtoon upsurge and tribal unrest on borders with Afghanistan above all tellingly underlines the peril of ignoring ethnic identities which are as powerful as religious identities. Its intensity has no doubt been aggravated by 'Kalashinkov culture', the role of the drug mafia and the state of law and order and democracy in that country. But essentially it was an ethnic violence which erupted for lack of other avenues of ethnic expression.

The term ethnic is here used as a broad non-religious identities based on race, culture, region, etc. Both the urges - religious and ethnic - provide the most vital clues to the political behaviour of the people of the subcontinent, including Muslims. Islam has nowhere inhibited the ethnic-cultural-nationalistic urges of its followers. The fact is evident from the existence of over forty sovereign nation states of Muslims in the world. The Quran itself recognized the ethnic identities of the Muslims when it said: "We created you in the form of tribes, so that you could be identified.

While Muslims, like any other community, have multiple identities, which identity, becomes pronounced at a particular time depends upon the situation at that time and which of them is perceived to be threatened.

Urdu speaking Muslims of the undivided India, who had once formed its ruling class, felt a threat to their religious identity from the possible domination of the Hindu majority after the withdrawal of the British. Their quest for a homeland became the genesis of the Pakistan movement and they comprised the vanguard of the movement and the Muslim League. Muslim communities in other areas where they were in a majority or had a pronounced regional characteristic, particularly in areas which now comprise Pakistan, did not respond enthusiastically to the League and its demand for Pakistan.

It was, in any case, a fatal underestimation of the ethnic urges of the Muslims by the Pakistan leadership that offended and alienated Kashmiri Muslims in 1947 and Bengali Muslims in 1971. For the same reason, the other four remaining ethnic communities of Pakistan had to be held together through a dictatorial regime.

The Urdu-speaking community became the most persecuted community after the emergence of ethnic identities in Pakistan. One manifestation of this emergence was the split of Pakistan and the birth of Bangladesh. The Biharis, as the Urdu-speaking community in Bangladesh is called, were the worst sufferers. Even now over two lakh of them are rotting in refugee camps whom neither Bangladesh is willing to rehabilitate nor Pakistan is willing to accept.

The Muhajirs were mostly settled in and around Karachi. They out-number Sindhis, Pathans and Punjabis in the city. About 8 lakh of Bihari migrants are concentrated in a single township of Orangi which was the scene of 1987 massacres. The hostility the Muhajirs had faced from Bangladeshis and Sindhis has now been excelled by the brutality of the Pathans.

The Pathans are another ethnic community of Pakistan which has not fully reconciled to their status in the country and the domination of Punjabis over them. In fact a large number of them led by leaders like Khan brothers had their reservation about the very idea of Pakistan. The Muhajir Pathan conflict dates back to 1965 when Field Marshal Ayub Khan supported by Pathans, won the presidential election against Fatama Jinnah, supported by the Muhajirs. Since then tension between two estranged communities seeking dominant position in Karachi city, has recurred often leading to violent clashes. The Muhajirs have been increasingly at the receiving end, particularly on account of their alienation from other Pakistanis also.

Indians and Pakistans are found to be far friendlier at ethnic-linguistic levels than at the national level. Punjabis, Sindhi and Urdu languages have been acting as emotional bridges between the two countries. Similarly Pathan and Baloach ethnic leaders were former stalwarts of the Indian freedom movement.

A better appreciation and empathy for the ethnic urges of people of Pakistan should help in developing cultural relation with them and in winning over their friendship which should inevitably be reflected in government relations as well.

The plight of the Urdu-speaking community in Bangladesh and Pakistan has also a direct bearing on the minds of its mainstream living in India. Its sub-continental affinities continue to exist. While these never amounted to extra-territorial loyalty, the community can no more look for emotional, moral or intellectual support across the border.

The realization of these facts has definitely encouraged a process of indigenisation of Indian Muslims. They are also becoming aware of their intellectual and cultural superiority to Muslims anywhere else in the world.

It does not, however, follow that Muslim alienation from the national mainstream has completely ended and that Hindu-Muslim relations have been restored to their ideal best. But it does follow that factors other than extra-territorial loyalty and transnational affinities of Indian Muslims might be responsible for the communal tangle. Indeed the growing assertion of the Muslims may be related to their awareness of their roots and rights in the country.

Moreover, Hindus, by and large, remain ignorant of the impact of the partition and developments in Pakistan on the Muslims of India and are still reacting to their preconceived perception of a monolithic Muslim mind of the pre-partition days. Intriguingly, emulative interest among the rest of the countrymen in Pakistan is proportional to the Muslim disillusionment with it.

The Sikh militants, for instance, seem in eighties directly inspired by what Muslim separatism is supposed to have achieved. But they did not realize how much damage the Muslims of India have done to their own interest by getting the country divided.

Similarly there is little realization in this country of the fact that refusal of Pakistan to recognize ethnic identities and its insistence on imposing a unitary form of government on a multi-ethnic nation have led to the demise of democracy and ethnic violence in that country.

A retreat from pluralism inspired by panic - which in turn is borne out of ignorance of the urges of sub-national identities - would not only undermine the basis of Indian unity and its democratic polity but also its role as a model of unity for the countries of the South Asia and as a source of inspiration for their ethnic identities.

Language, culture and region which comprise our definition of ethnic identities are the only potent rival of religious identities and hence the most powerful secularizing influence on the Indian polity. But instead of encouraging a community like Muslims to get integrated with other communities at the regional level, where they not only share a common language, culture, history, heroes saints and other symbols, they are expected to merge into an elusive mainstream and conform to an arbitrarily fixed standard of nationalism.

By ignoring the ethnic dimension of Muslims, they are being forcibly monolithised. Kashmir is usually treated more as a Muslim problem than a Kashmiri problem. Promotion of Urdu is treated more as a concession to the Muslim community than as a cultural need of a vital ethnic identity of which it is the mother tongue. And when attempts at monolithisation of the community are accompanied by attempts at its homogenization with the majority, communal tensions are bcund to develop.

Policy towards minorities in India has often oscillated between 'toughness' and 'appeasement.' As long as these policies are not based on correct understanding of their urges, neither can succeed. What is needed is a more intelligent policy with a view to finding out the extent to which the urges of the minority are compatible with those of the majority and the national interest.

Muslim urges include urges of multiple identities of the community; partly shared with others and partly exclusive. What should be the legitimate field and degree of autonomy of an exclusive religious identity in a secular country is a question which would be more fruitfully debated and decided with the knowledge that Indian Muslims are, emotionally or intellectually, not dependent on any other country and have the potentiality of becoming a source of inspiration for Muslims elsewhere. In fact the whole question of transnational identities should be treated as an opportunity of opening bridges of friendship and understanding with neighbouring countries. In any case, a policy for dealing with the urges of such identities should be a vital component of the defence and diplomatic policy of the country.

The current turmoil in Pakistan is an occasion for fresh thinking on a wide range of problems in India including its Pakistan policy, Hindu-Muslim relations, role of ethnic identities in national integration and opportunities and challenges of transnational identities. The occasion reminds that ideological, cultural and moral components of the nation's power are as important as physical might. And that while neither the urge for religious identities should be underestimated nor should the fears about it be exaggerated. No people, including Muslims, live by religion alone.

(*Economic* & *Political Weekly*, Vol. XX/L No.4, January 24, 1987)

6

Mohammad Iqbal and the Universe of Muslim Identities

This paper is an attempt at revisiting the universe of identities of Muslims of India, conceptualized by me earlier,[1] in the august company of Mohammad Iqbal; and to acknowledge Iqbal's influence in shaping and sharpening these identities.

As I viewed it, Muslims of India simultaneously belong to four broad vertical levels of identities-international, sub-continental, national and regional-in addition to several other horizontal identities like those of class, profession, ideology, party and so on. They share some of these identities with other communities. The degree of allegiance of these identities varies from person to person and situation to situation. In fact identities proliferate to meet the needs of a growing personality. As a family grows, a man simultaneously becomes a son, a brother, a husband and a father. Tagore explains the same idea by citing the analogy of a seed which has a single identity, but which as it blossoms forth into a flower gets differentiated into petals and leaves.

Iqbal is not entirely unaware of various dimensions of Muslim identity. But his emphasis on one dimension at a time does give the impression of exclusiveness on this account. In his own time and perception, the nature of Muslim identity did vary. But far more drastic changes have taken place after him. Some allowance must also be made for the inadequacies of his sociological tools. For he did not aspire to be a social scientist or a coherent system builder. He belongs to the genre of prophets whose mission is to translate his vision to reality. In that role also he had to grapple with the task of reconciling the diverse facets of reality as he perceived them.

Islamic Umma

Iqbal reiterates the obvious when he underlines the cosmopolitan character of the Islamic Umma transcending time and space. There is hardly any other faith that inspires so much international solidarity among its followers as Islam does. And it is the Muslim community of the sub-continent that "today leads the Muslims of the World in their zeal and practical behaviours for the spread of their faith".[2]

There are three main aspects of the international community of Muslim: political, ideological and cultural. At the political level, Pan-Islamic ideas reflect the urge for unification of the Muslims under Islamic World Government. Traditionally, Pan-Islamism has been an ally of Indian nationalism. The Khilafat movement was an outstanding example of the alliance. Gandhi invested his entire political and emotional power on it to enlist Muslim support for the national cause. A staunch nationalist like M A Ansari considered Pan-Islamism "the most sacred and exalted passion of Muslims". Even today Pan-Islamic tendencies do not clash with the interests of Indian nationalism. Both had, for instance, adopted the non-aligned framework in world politics.

Iqbal, on the other hand, was sceptical about the unification of Muslims of the world into a single political state and even rejected the contention that Jamalud-Din Afghani was ever associated with this 'dream'. He, in fact, suspected that the idea was planted by the British to divert attention of the Muslims of India from internal political questions and to "dissipate their power of action by lip sympathy with the Muslim world".[3] He considered it significant that "in no Islamic language - Arabic, Persian or Turkish - does there exist a phrase corresponding to Pan-Islamism".

On Khilafat also, Iqbal was less sentimental than most of its Hindu and Muslim supporters. He rather believed that spirit of Islam was at work through Attaturk who abolished the Khilagat.[4] He criticised religious scholars of Islam in India for not appreciating Turkish view which according to him was "perfectly sound".[5] In any case this ideal, according to him, had become ineffective and could no more be used as a vital force in the reorganisation of Islam. He also noted that "the international ideal of Islam had been hitherto overshadowed or rather displaced by Arabian imperialism of earlier centuries of Islam".[6]

One of the unambiguous exponents of the ideological aspect of Islam is Jamat-I-Islami. Maulana Maudoodi, the founder of the Jamaat, rejected the concept of Muslim nationalism which he regarded as Un-Islamic and vicious as Indian nationalism. According to Maudoodi, the ideology of Islam could be threatened as much by 'Munafeqeen' within the Muslim community as by outsiders.

Iqbal's views are in glaring contrast with those of the Jamaat. His basic concern is the Muslim community. In order to meet its growing needs, he even attempted a 'revision' and 'reconstruction' of religious thought in Islam. "Even the most orthodox mullah has no right to expel anybody from Islam as long as he has faith in its two basic principles: Tauheed (oneness of God) and finality of Mohammad's prophethood".[7] To him social polity of Islam was more important than its theology. In order to make Islam a living force in the world of today, Iqbal insisted on the need of Ijtehad (innovation in religious thought) and of satisfying cultural urges of its followers. "For being a live member of the Muslim community unconditional faith in Islam is not enough. One must imbibe its culture as well."[8] The objective of his Persian poems, Iqbal said, was not advocacy of Islam; his urge and quest were concentrated on finding "a modern polity".

In his search for a viable basis of the international level of Muslim identity, Iqbal lay special emphasis on its cultural component. Culture, for Iqbal, included history, sociology, literature, fine arts, crafts, etc. He makes ecstatic references to the past glory and achievements of Muslims in these fields and some of his finest poetry is inspired by those themes. Indeed, Niaz Fatehpuri complained that Iqbal was concerned, not so much with Islam and its ethical teachings as with Islamic history and Islamic conquests.

On this point, Iqbal is also vulnerable to attacks from Jamaat-I-Islami school of thought on the one hand and from nationalists and secular liberals on the other. Thomas Arnold has noted that "there is little peculiarly Islamic in contributions which Occidental and Oriental Muslims have made... The arts and sciences that comprise the legacy were those that flourished under the protection and patronage of the Islamic empires".[9] Firaq Gorakhpuri similarly argues that religion and culture are not synonymous. If Germany or England or America is converted to Islam, their culture would not become the Hajazi culture.

Iqbal anticipates this sort of criticism and makes ample concession to it. The concepts of the East and the West, recurring throughout his poetry, clearly imply acceptance of close inter-connection of geography and culture. The potentiality of Islam, according to him, lies in the fact that on account of its geographical location. It is the meeting ground of the East and the West.

Iqbal also traces racial components of Islamic culture. While conceding that the Arabs, who gave birth to Islam, contributed to its political evolution, he also takes note of the valuable contribution of non-Arabs in the field of arts and sciences, philosophy and medicine. He considers Iran as the single greatest factor in the growth of Islamic culture and civilization. "Our Islamic Culture is a by-product of the mixture of Semitic thought and Aryan speculation...It got its subtlety and charm from the womb of its Aryan mother and inherited its dignity and forbearance from its Semitic father."[10] Iqbal's concept of Islamic culture, however, has a West Asian orientation and is not universal enough to include, say African Islam or Indonesian Islam. Thus while Iqbal does not believe in a monolithic political or ideological basis of the international Muslim community, he fails to project a monolithic cultural basis for it either. Racial, territorial and other factors diversity it also.

Territorial Identities

As the sub-continental, national and regional identities-to which Muslims of India simultaneously belong-are forms of territorial identity and as sub-continental identity of today is synonymous with Indian identity of Iqbal's time, his views on territorial loyalties should be relevant to all the three discussed here.

Intriguingly Iqbal outgrew the concept of nationalism and used the West Asian model of Islam to undermine it at a time when resurgence of territorial nationalism was sweeping across that region. He tries to resolve the dilemma by conceding that Islam and nationalism can be reconciled where Muslims are in a majority and where the two are practically synonymous. He further acknowledge the reality of non-religious basis of identity which diversifies Muslims also. He dispels the impression that Islam is opposed to racial identities as such and quotes the Quranic verse which says; "we created you in the form of tribes so that you could be identified".[11]

Again, in his reply to the criticism of Maulana Hussain Ahmad Madani, who maintained that nations were based on country and not religion, Iqbal concedes that the Quran used the world Umma and not nation for Muslims. But he merely asserts that the status of Umma is superior to that of the nation. Nor is he unmindful of the legitimate obligations that the citizens owe to nationalism. "If nationalism means patriotism and sacrifice of one's life for the honour of one's country, such nationalism is a part of Muslim faith."[12]

Iqbal was even confident of harmonising religion and patriotism in India provided cultural entity of Muslim could be preserved. Addressing the Muslim League Session in 1930, he said that "Muslims of India would not spare greatest sacrifices for the freedom of their country if their right to autonomous growth within the country under their own traditions and culture was conceded."[13] Concretely, Iqbal suggested at that stage reorganisation of the country on the basis of language, race, history, religion and economic interests within the Indian federal system with maximum autonomy for the states. In order to preserve Muslim identity and create a Muslim centre of political power he wanted amalgamation of North Western states of Punjab, Frontier, Sind and Baluchistan into one State within India and demanded one third representation to Muslims of the rest of the country in the federal legislature. Such a formula, Iqbal felt, would strengthen sense of responsibility and patriotism among the Muslims and that they would prove best defenders of the borders of India against foreign threats-armed or ideological. After Muslims were ensured against the fear of Hindu domination through his formula and after the British left the country, Iqbal believed that "Islam in India would be able to rid itself of the influence of Arab imperialism and thus end the stagnation that had shackled its civilization, culture, shariat and education for centuries."[14]

Iqbal thus did not want uniqueness compromised either in the name of nationalism (Indian) or of Islam (represented by Arabia). He made a significant contribution to the creation of a sense of pride, identity and mission among the Muslims of the sub-continent. He believed in the special destiny of the community which was the greatest Muslim community of the world in his time. For according to him "it is no exaggeration to say that India is the only country of the world where unifying potentialities of Islam got its finest expression". The interests of the sub-continental Muslims were foremost in his mind and his appeal was primarily addressed to them. He was not only a proud Indian (sub-continental) Muslim but also a proud Indian and wished the two positions to be reconciled.

Somehow, the conditions propounded by Iqbal for reconciling Indian nationalism and Muslim identity could not be met. The debate on whether or not and how far he was responsible for the creation of Pakistan is generally coloured by a desire to credit him for the 'achievement' or exonerate him from (or blame him for) the 'guilt'.

The fact is that ideologically he represents Pakistan much less though culturally much more–than other leaders of the movement. Islam is certainly the most vital component of the region for which he demanded a separate state and which now broadly comprises Pakistan. But Nanak and Ram Tirath are not aliens to this region as they were not to his poetry. It was this region which he wanted to protect from 'Hindu domination' as well as 'Arab imperialism'. A Pakistani writer recently shared his fears of the threat from the West as according to him, Iran and Saudi Arabia are "competing for the soul of Pakistan."

Iqbal spelled his ideas more clearly in his letter to Jinnah dated June 21, 1937 in which he suggested a separate federation of Muslim provinces. The crucial point is not whether this federation could be formed and preserved within India, but the fact that he was demanding a right of self-determination for a particular territorial culture and not a homeland for the entire Muslim community of the sub-continent. He specifically and significantly advised Jinnah "to ignore Muslim minority provinces". And underlined the importance of holding of a North West Indian Muslim Conference.

The implications of the two approaches are clear. If Muslims of the present India had been excluded from the campaign of Pakistan, as advised by Iqbal, the relations between the two communities and between the two countries would have been far more normal. Pakistan would then have been essentially a cultural and territorial entity instead of hopelessly aspiring to represent the urges of the Muslims of the entire sub-continent.

His son Javeed Iqbal is not far wrong in believing that if his logic was extended and had he been alive till the creation of Pakistan he would have founded another concept and called it Pakistani nationalism.[15] Those who call Pakistan a living mausoleum of Iqbal overlook the fact that a part of him is still vital enough to influence the controversy on the basic character of the State of Pakistan; whereas a part of him is sub-continental, another is universal beyond any mausoleum.

The sub-continental dimension of the identity of Muslims of India has undoubtedly survived the partition of the sub-continent. Iqbal, who was a prominent champion of this entity, continues to be one of its symbols and sources of inspiration. The identity has other deep emotional, cultural, racial and historical roots as well.

However, in the common sub-continental identity, Indian part of Muslim population apprehended that they would to be treated as a poor relation. According to Javeed Iqbal, the split in the freedom movement of India led to the parting of ways of Islam and India, the implication is that India is or would be without Islam.[16] I H Qureshi pessimistically predicted that "in a hundred years, perhaps in a shorter time, the Muslim people may cease to exist in India."[17] In his characteristic consistency and forthrightness Jamat-I-Islami leader Maulana Maudoodi, on migration to Pakistan, left the following advice for his followers in India: "we have nothing to do with the government and its administration and should assure Hindu nationalism by their attitude that there is no other political nationality in the field to fight it".[18] He conceded that India should be a Hindu State.

Notwithstanding the consequences of the brute logic of the partition for the Muslims of India, if not for the sub-continental Muslim identity, W C Smith believed, as early as in 1957, that "Islam in India would emerge more progressive, dynamic, liberal and creative than Pakistani Islam".[19]

Its South Eastern links are an additional advantage. Development in Pakistan reinforce this trend. Vocal champions of what are called Pak-Indians are already asserting their cultural links with the Indo-Islamic civilization. Other Pakistanis are also unlikely to have remained completely uninfluenced by, say, achievements of Indian federalism, democracy and economy.

This is not to deny that in terms of political power, Indian Muslims are not as important as they would have been in the united India or as they are in the other two countries of the sub-continent. But political satisfaction of a community also depends on the class or group that exercises power on its behalf and the amount of political freedom its individual members enjoy. Moreover, if Iqbal is right in emphasizing the role of cultural factors in the growth of Islam, Indian Muslims have obvious advantages. However, it is difficult to draw much upon Iqbal in discussing the sub-continental identity of Indian Muslims as they were not divided into two nations in his life-time and he could not have anticipated their problems after division. But if Pakistani nationalists and Pakistani Muslims insist on monopolizing him, they would deprive themselves of a vital link with the sub-continental identity at their own cost.

Iqbal and Indian Nationalism

What are the legitimate forms through which the Muslim identity should manifest itself in the national life? What should be the relations of this identity with the national identity?

Can we go to Iqbal for an answer to these questions? Could he have reconciled to the reality of Indian nationalism, having recognized nationalism of Turkey, Iran, Arab States and, by implication, of Pakistan? As Pakistan, according to Iqbal, was to be a movement of self-determination for the cultural entity of the North-west, he did not expect Muslims of the rest of India to own this culture or the movement. If this advice had been heeded they would have been spared of the tragic embarrassment they had to suffer at the time of the partition and would have achieved a far better adjustment with the claims of Indian nationalism. He himself was proud of his Indian and even Brahmanic origin. "I am sprung from the same stock; India is older than Hinduism and Islam, and will remain when we and our creeds have become one with Yesterday's seven thousand years. However, in the context of the situation then prevailing, he also justified the right of Muslims, if they were in a minority, to seek autonomy as a cultural identity. But he did not work out the form and quantum of this autonomy. He was silent about relations of Muslims and non-Muslims even if it were possible for the former to acquire a political unity in the world, let history answer this question, he said.[20]

As Iqbal concedes legitimacy to nationalism in Muslim majority countries but is not clear about its concept where Muslims are merely a partner in it, there is a case for Ijtehad in his concept of nationalism for country like India. The question of the status of the Muslim identity in India must therefore be discussed in the wider context of relations of the national identity with numerous intermediary identities between an individual and the nation. It might necessitate a clearer definition of nationalism itself.

Iqbal has often been called Marx of the East and the first Islamic Socialist. There is much in his writings which gives comfort to the socialist minds and can be called a clarion call to workers, peasants and other exploited classes. He is also believed to have expressed his dissatisfaction with the class character of the Muslim League. But none of these facts is directly relevant to know his attitude towards an identity based on class.

However, he does specifically suggest that struggle for amelioration of the economic condition of the people should be on completely non-religious lines. "Anybody who aspires to resolve this problem should keep his mind completely free of all religious and communal differences."[21] Even if leaders of different communities cannot agree on other matters, they should pool their heads at least on economic matters and think of measures for the common welfare of the country. This is a significant and categoric acceptance of the desirability of class identity which Muslims should agree with non-Muslims. As economic issues form a major part of political ideologies, alignments on non-communal lines for economic issues pleaded by Iqbal would have serious implications for political and ideological alignments of communities

It is generally suggested by many secularists that religious communities might retain their autonomy in social and cultural fields but not in politics. There are certain obvious limits beyond which social life cannot be compartmentalized. Sports, films and entertainment cannot and should not be segregated on religious lines. The limits within which religious identities do manifest are confined to religious rituals and festivals. However, within these limits we could conceive of a sub-identity of Muslims within the social identity.

The real controversy centres round the political role of Muslims as a community. But just as there cannot be complete autonomy in social and cultural fields for Muslims or any other religious community, such autonomy cannot be completely denied to them in the political field, leaving aside the various means-constitutional, institutional, formal and informal-through which Muslim identity can or should seek recognition and autonomy in India, I confine my observations mostly to what Iqbal has said explicitly or implicitly on the subject.

Iqbal had in mind some sort of dual federal polity, territorial as well as religious. But he did not work out the details and implications of the latter. For a mere fixation of quota for the community (which in the context of his own time he fixed at 33 per cent in the central legislature) does not ensure share in political power.

A more serious difficulty would arise in defining how far religion and politics can be separated in a government in which Muslims and non-Muslims are participants; how far modern legislation be made independent of the traditional sources of jurisprudence.

Iqbal definitely suggests that the power of ijtehed be transferred from Ulama to the legislature. But he was aware of the difficulties this suggestion might create in a country like India where the legislature would include non-Muslims also. While discussing the issue in another context, he conceded that "concept of separation of church and state is not altogether unknown to Islam."[22] But this separation, he hastened to add, was essentially that of functions and not of beliefs.

Again, referring to the rejection by Turkey of the old ideas about the function of State and Religion which accentuated the separation of church and State, he maintained that the structure of Islam as a religio-political system did permit such a view. All that he insisted was that the State should not be more dominant and rule all other ideas embodied in the system of Islam. In Islam, the nature of an act, however, secular in its import, was determined by the attitude with which the agent does it.

This is a perfectly logical position. For while the subjects may be divided-the person dealing with them must have an integrated mind. It is conceivable that people deriving inspiration from different sources agree on some common socio-economic and other ideological issues. It is an agreement on such issues that is the basis of a political identity called party. Iqbal has already conceded non-communal approach on economic issues. It would not grossly violate Iqbalian framework it the list of such issues is enlarged.

His assurance to "respect from his heart for the laws, rites and cultural and religious institutions"[23] of other communities indicates a further scope of flexibility in his stand. As the concept of Indian secularism does not preclude belief in religion and only insists on respect for all religions, Iqbal might not be as far away from it as he seems.

However, instead of stretching the logic of Iqbal to fit into the concept of modern secular state, some ijtehad (innovation) may be necessary in Iqbal's thoughts in view of the drastically changed situation since his time, in the same spirit in which he used to subject religious thoughts to ijtehad. There are many formal and informal arrangements in operation for working out a system of what may be called a multiple federation; a federation of regions, cultures, communities, castes, classes, ideologies and so on superimposed as well as cutting across one another. Many more constitutional and institutional innovations are possible and necessary to preserve various identities and provide them a sense of participation in the national affairs.

(Economics and Political Weekly, February 21, 1981)

Notes

1. Earlier chapters.
2. Murray T Titus, *"Islam in India of Iqbal"*.
3. Shamloo, "*Statements and Speeches of Iqbal*".
4. Tassaduq Hussain Taj, "*Mazamin Iqbal*", Hyderabad, p. 171.
5. Iqbal, "*Reconstruction of Religious Thought in Islam*", Lahore, p. 157.
6. Ibid, p. 158.
7. Tassaduq Hussain Taj, op cit, p. 169.
8. Ibid, p. 91.
9. Thomas Arnold, "*Legacy of Islam*"
10. Tassaduq Hussain Taj op cit, p. 90.
11. *Ibid*, p. 174.
12. *Ibid,* p. 189-90.
13. *Ibid,* p. 178.
14. *Ibid.*
15. Javeed Iqbal, "*Stray Reflections*".
16. Javeed Iqbal, op cit.
17. Quoted by Mion Shakir in "*Muslims in Free India*".
18. *Radiance*, December 17, 1960.
19. W C Smith, "*Islam in Modern History*".
20. Quoted by S Sinha, "*Iqbal: The Poet and His Message*", p. 34.
21. Tassaduq Hussain Taj, op. cit, p. 104.
22. *Ibid.*
23. *Ibid.*

7

Urdu and Muslim Identity

Redefining Urdu Politics in India Edited by Ather Farouqui, Oxford, pp. 309.

Nineteen eminent scholars, belonging to different disciplines, including foreigners, commissioned by Ather Farouqui join in an exercise in Redefining Urdu Politics in India, in the form of a book with this title.

Many among them do not know Urdu. But all of them are friends of Urdu. A majority of them are non-Muslims (twelve in number). But all of them are friends of Muslims. Thus they cannot be accused of a bias against Urdu and Muslims when they hold, with varying emphasis that both have not received a fair deal in independent India. It is not possible to even give a brief summary of every view point or to quote every author in the book. There are inevitable repetitions and some contradictions in a volume of such a nature. Broadly it covers three main questions. First, what is the relations between Muslims and Urdu or need a religious community have a language of its own? Second, how far Urdu has declined in the land of its birth and what are its causes? Third, what remedial measures are needed and what is the possible role of non-Muslims in the revival process?

I belong to an age and place—Jammu—when and where Urdu was a language of administration, religious and political discourse, public speaking and journalism. Lahore Urdu press which covered my region represented all view points, from extremist Hindus to extremist Muslims and moderates in between. I started my public career as editor of an Urdu weekly in 1942 and had read religious books like Ramayan and Mahabharat in Urdu as Barbara D.Metcalf observes, "the early tracts of Hindu revival movements like Ariya Samaj were written in Urdu."

As a language of literature Urdu reigned supreme in the entire north India. Its importance lies in the development of literary and cultural tradition of India." Its secular character was so pronounced that "Muslim Ulama considered Urdu literature as Kufr" (p. 27). Ralf Russel quotes Ashraf. Thanvi, who in his famous book *Bhishti Zewar* presented a long list of literary books that he considered as Kufr. Needless to add that most of these were masterpieces of literature. Only a great Urdu poet like Mir could say "you may break kaaba but do not break human heart." Or sample the following couplet of Zauq, Ustad of last Mughal emperor Bahadurshah Zafar :

Zauq jo madresey ke biggarey huey hain mullah

un ko maikhaaney mein lay aao sanvar jayengey.

(Zauq these mullah who have been spoilt in madrasas,

Bring them to tavern and they will be put right.)

On the issue of present condition of Urdu the authors in the book under review share a common concern. But on the precise nature of this condition and the causes thereof, views vary. Barbara D. Metcalf recognises Urdu's role as transnational language as also language of communication between different communities and of the market. She also refers to popularity of Urdu Ghazal and its dominance in Indian films. Apart from dialogue and songs which are invariably in Urdu, the titles of films like *Kabhi Alvida Na Kehna, Zakham, Salam-e-Istaq, Fana and Fida*—to name only very recent releases—are in pure Urdu. Just a cursory look at hit songs of some recent so called Hindi films confirm the fact that their language is nothing but Urdu. A few illustrations would suffice. Shabe firaq hai (Chupke Chupke), Zaherin fazle rabbi (zindagi), Ya Ali (Gangster) and Khala hai seene me ik (Jism).

But as Rashid Banarsi laments, "you can write Urdu and call it Hindi. In films all the language is Urdu but they are given Hindi certificates (p. I06)." Indeed Hindi wallas own Urdu as one of its shally (styles). Of course, in their diction and grammar, the two languages are similar to each other.

Colin Masica calls the Urdu-Hindi relationship as "the ultimate anamoly." They are, he says, not even different dialects in a linguistic sense (Masica 1991, p. 27). But why as a superior language, Urdu could not claim Hindi to be part of it? Why nobody ever raised the issue of calling Urdu films as Hindi films? But who can object if Urdu writers, particularly poets, have a far better market in Devenagri script than Hindi writers have got? Urdu's claim to be the language of a composite nation in favour of an exclusive Muslim language received a set back when the two nations theory was propounded by the Muslims League and Urdu was claimed to be the language of the Muslim nation, though barely 4 per cent people in what became Pakistan could speak the language in 1947.

The case for Hindustani—a common language in two scripts- as the official language to which the Congress was committed suffered after independance. Hindi was unanimously accepted by the Constituent Assembly of India as the official language. Not even a single member - Hindu or Muslim—voted against it. Thus the partition, observes Yoginder Singh, "came as a serious blow to the Indian Muslims (and Urdu). A large number of elite, middle class and enterpreneurial populace migrated to Pakistan... It also made most Muslims guilty at a time when the constitution was adopted." He adds, the Muslims leadership suffered from an identity crisis. "The debate among some Muslim intellectuals on whether Urdu should shed its Arabic, Persian script exemplifies this crisis." However, Gandhi was the lone voice of dissent on that occasion. In his letter dated January 11, 1948, just 19 days before he was shot dead, he reiterated his view that "both Devanagri and Urdu be jointly recognised as the national script." Even Prime Minister Nehru bemoaned, a decade after independence, the condition of Urdu in a state like Urdu which "is its best known and the most spoken language and home of Amir Khusru, Ghalib and Khan-i-Khana". He added, "most people, like tonga walas, taxi drivers, etc., know Urdu much more than any other language and they are rather lost when the signboards are not in Urdu."

(Selected works of Jawaharlal Nehru, second series, 1 August - 31 August 1957).

Language has many uses-a means of communication, an instrument of transmitting knowledge and expression of cultural and creative urges of a community. But it is what Robert King calls iconic use of language that creates its own problems. According to Pratap Bhanu Mehta, "at one level an iconic use of language can be liberating". But he thinks that as a marker of an identity Urdu has suffered disadvantages. However, Yoginder Singh argues that" the Urdu language has, over the years, assumed a significant space in the structure of Muslims identity in India. The issue of cultural identity has appropriated the maximum space of legitimacy with regard to the Urdu language." He, therefore, concludes, that "Urdu education has to take into consideration the social, cultural, economic and political aspirations of the Muslims community."

I remember that while addressing an Urdu conference, I had provoked my audience, some decades back by the remark that the next generation of Urdu knowing Hindus, including of eminent Urdu writers, was becoming ignorant of the language and that the time might not be far off when it would become language of Muslims. In those days every Urdu conference that I attended spent considerable time to assert that Urdu was not the language of Muslims and represented composite cultural heritage of India.

Notwithstanding past claims and realities about Urdu, any discussion on Muslim problem today invariably would include the state of Urdu.

Sachar Committee, appointed by the Prime Minister to report on the status of Muslims, for instance, could not ignore the problems of Urdu.

It is in this context that "madrasas have assumed importance as repositories of Urdu education p. 150". On account of lack of arrangement for Urdu teaching in government schools, parents who want their children to learn Urdu have to send them to the madrasas. They provide cheap education to the poor Muslims who may not otherwise be able to afford it. There are, therefore, half a million madrasas where fifty million full time students are getting almost free education. While many of the suspicions about madrasas being breeding ground of fundamentalists and potential terrorists may be too wild and exaggerated and a number of measures to modernise them are being taken by the government. Urdu is more a medium of religious instruction than that of literature. The rich secular literary and cultural heritage of the language is thus being diluted in madrasa education.

However, the government has set up Urdu academies in most of the states where Muslims are in sufficient number to satisfy demand of Muslims. While Urdu is being accessible to more and more Muslim communities, it is being neglected in Urdu speaking areas. The meeting of the National Minority Committee held on July 10 and 11, 2006, for instance, decided to open Urdu medium schools where the population of Muslims is more than 16 per cent. Strongly reacting to this decision, Syed Iqbal Hasnain, Vice Chancellor of the University of Calicut, Kerala, asks, "how will this be implemented in Kerala's Mallapuram, a Muslim majority district where not a single soul knows a word of Urdu?" (*Asian Age*, October 10, 2006).

It may be true that most of the Urdu reading (not speaking) persons are by now Muslims. But not all Muslims are Urdu reading or speaking. The latter presumption would be as fatal for the cause of Urdu and Muslims as was the claim of Muslims being a separate nation and Urdu being their language.

Urdu speaking Muslims, therefore, must aspire, in cooperation with non-Muslim lovers of Urdu, to preserve the rich composite cultural heritage of Urdu and not be content with its being a mere medium of acquiring religious knowledge. Instead of complaining that Hindi was appropriating this heritage, as pointed out above, its cooperation should be sought. A suggestion made by, besides others, Syed Shahabuddin for a composite Hindi-Urdu course is very pertinent in this context. A capsule course of best Hindi and Urdu literature could be introduced at higher secondary level in what is called Hindi region.

Similarly much ground for teaching of technical subject and for higher education must be yielded to English. For no Indian languages, not to speak of Urdu, is equipped for that. The minimum aim for the children of Urdu speaking persons should be as one author has put it, their alphabetisation in their mother tongue. While the recommendation of the Sachar Committee to increase the fund of the Maulana Azad Education Foundation to Rs 1000 crore may be welcome, more important and easier to implement would be to extend facilities for Urdu medium primary education. It is most surprising ever mischievous to twist the three language formula in the North India to exclude Urdu as an optional language. Apart from compulsory education in Hindi, as the regional language and English as a modem Europen languages, the students are required to take Sanskrit as the third language. By no stretch of logic Sanskrit is more important than Urdu, for those whose mother tongue is Urdu, for primary education.

What is needed is clarity about the role of Urdu, as literacy in the mother tongue of Urdu speaking children, and in promotion of national culture. The present book provides an excellent basis for a discussion of this role.

Milli Gazette 16-31 May, 2007.

8

Problems and Opportunities of Urdu Speaking Muslims

The terrorist attack on Samjhauta Express on Feburary 18, 2007 was generally interpreted in terms of relations between India and Pakistan and was condemned as an attack on peace process between the two countries, by their leaders as also of many other countries. Tony Blair, Prime Minister of Great Britain, however, betrayed his ignorance when he condemned what he called "a wicked act" and considered "it interesting that the train was a symbol of Hindus and Muslims working together." He missed the reality that there are more Muslims in India than in Pakistan and who have, on the whole, been loyal to their country and supported it in its conflicts with Pakistan.

While it is likely that the blast was handiwork of those interested in sabotaging the peace process going on between India and Pakistan, it, above all, highlighted the continued plight of Urdu speaking Muslims in the two countries. The 70 victims of the tragedy were mostly Muslims of India and Pakistan belonging to this community and the train is mainly used by members of its divided families who travel to meet them on either sides

Some years back I met MQM (Muhajir Qaumi Mahaz) leaders in London. I told them that while I conceded that a girl's loyalty, after her marriage should be to her in laws, her emotional and cultural ties with her parent's home need not be snapped. My analogy appealed to them very much as it aptly summed up their dilemma. They confessed that their cultural roots lay in India—in Ganga-Jamuna belt. The urge to belong to their roots was becoming stronger and stronger over the years. I might have to amend the analogy somewhat because since then I have met some families in which husband and wife continue to proclaim separate national identities. In a recent programme on an Indian channel, an Indian woman says that her first condition for a marriage with a Pakistani man was that she would retain her Indian identity. Their young son said that he belonged to the two nations and was an Indian Pakistani. As Muslims of the subcontinent often marry their close cousins, who, in case of Urdu speaking Muslims belong to two countries, this is their peculiar problem.

Dilemma of Urdu speaking Muslims has its own specificity, different from the Muslim problem viewed from global, sub-continental, historical and macro angles which are often oversimplified.

The community has lost its political and cultural clout in India as its elite migrated to Pakistan in 1947 where, too, it lost its importance after a few years when important leaders of Pakistan, from India, passed away and local communities like Punjabis, Sindhis, Pathans and Balochs asserted their identity. In all the three countries, into which they were divided - India, Pakistan and Bangladesh - the community faces a similar crisis of identity and a similar charge.

It suffered a worse fate in Bangladesh which does not forgive it for opposing its struggle for liberation. Local communities of Pakistan do not forgive it for its continued nostalgia for the land of its origin. Many Indian Hindus have not quite forgiven it for having demanded the partition of the country.

Muhajir Qaumi Mahaz (MQM) leader Altaf Hussain, who represents Urdu speaking community in Pakistan, called Muhajirs during his visit to India a few year back, thus rightly observed that the partition of India was the greatest blunder in human history. For, it divided the Urdu speaking Muslim community among whom the movement of the partition had maximum support, into three countries.

Notwithstanding its present plight, the community had a unique geo-historical entity. Drawn from diverse ethnic stocks, it was homogenized and indegenised by a common political role and powerful Urdu culture. Under the impact of the two greatest civilizations of the world, i.e., ancient Indian and modem Western, its intellectual and cultural attainments are almost unparalleled by any other Muslim community of the world. Though a minority in its own region, it materially shaped the religious and political role of Islam in the entire sub-continent.

In its hey day, the community shared power with the non-Muslim elite of the heartland region of India, which no other Muslim community is known to have done elsewhere, and with its help subjugated Muslim communities around like those of Kashmir, North West and Bengal in the name of extending the frontiers of Hindustan. Even today folk tradition of these peripheral regions regards Mughals as aggressors. Some of the Hindu rulers also revolted against the Central authority. But revolts of both communities were more regional than religions.

The Mughals and the Urdu-speaking Muslim aristocracy came to represent not only the central authority but also a spirit of pan-Indian patriotism. It was therefore not an accident that Bahadurshah Zafar was the natural choice for leadership of the first war of India's independence in 1857 in which 70 per cent 50,000 soldiers who revolted were caste Hindus. The end of the Mughal empire was a traumatic experience for the ruling Muslim elite. From a dominant community of the heartland, it stepped into the role of a leading elite of the pan-India Muslim community. But in its new role, it could not settle terms with the emergent Indian nationalism, defined in Hindu religious idiom and with the expanding role of the more numerous community of the Hindus in the national stream.

Separate homeland

Gandhi tried to redefine Indian Muslim identity in Pan-Islamic terms, by leading the Khilafat movement.But its collapses in Turkey, the King of which claimed to be the head of the Muslim world for the survival of which Gandhi had launched a movement supported by the Muslim Ulama. It is obvious that the identity problem was not so acute for those Muslims who were in a majority. But minority Muslim communities of which the Urdu-speaking community was the most vocal, sought an answer to their identity urge in a separate homeland.

Far from consolidating the Muslim identity, the formation of Pakistan split it and the worst victim of the split was the Urdu-speaking community. Its dilemma was tellingly demonstrated during the Indo-Pak wars of 1965 and 1971 when it learnt what it meant to be divided into two-and later three-different nation states with conflicting claims of patriotism. Loyalties of the community were heavily strained.

The people who comprise the present Pakistan were never too deeply enthused by its ideology. The Muhajirs as the Urdu-speaking migrants to Pakistan are called were at that time the most faithful followers of that ideology. They supported the Muslim League and later the Jamaat-I-Islami to demonstrate their belief in the primacy of religious identity and disapproval of ethnic, linguistic and regional loyalties. Those who were in the then 'eastern wing of Pakistan' never wavered in their loyalty to united Pakistan during the revolt of Bangladesh. But while Bangladesh treated them as traitors, Pakistan refused to accept them. They are thus stateless citizens in Bangladesh. Ironically, loyalty of the other part of the same community who had migrated to the western wing of Pakistan also came to be suspected by every other community there.

A liberal Pathan leader like Wali Khan, during his visit to India said, that if Muhajirs were unable to adjust themselves in Pakistan, they should return to the country of their origin. A Sindhi leader, Pir Ahmad Bux had retorted that if Urdu wallahs had their way and India was willing to admit them, Karachi would overnight be denuded of 70 percent of its population". A Sindhi daily Hilal-e-Pakistan described them as "virtual Indian agents who should be sent to India".

Having come to clash with other Pakistani nationalities separately, now a joint Punjabi-Pathan front is threatening their physical existence in Karachi where most of them are settled. Ethnic assertion of others, says the Muhajir Qaumi Mahaz leader Khalid Sultan, "made us aware that we have a separate, cultural, historical and linguistic identity from other nationalities of Pakistan". Having failed to discover an Islamic melting pot in which all ethnic identities would dissolve, the Muhajirs too demanded their recognition as one of the five nationalities of Pakistan and a separate homeland within the country which they called Urdu-Pradesh, to revive their nostalgia for U.P. the land of their origin.

Nostalgia for the mother country and a sense of pride for their roots are becoming as powerful among the Muhajir as among any other Indian community settled abroad. Rais Amrohi, the doyen of Pak-Indians, as he preferred to call his community, was proud of the fact that "our ancestors gave to the sub-continent one of the greatest civilizations of the world". He is equally proud of the delta land between the Ganga and the Jamuna on which flourished "the great edifice of the Indo-Islamic civilization". If four other nationalities like Punjabis, Pathans, Sindhis and Balouchs can claim their homeland in Pakistan, Rais Amrohi asked, "What is wrong in the demand of Pak-Indians for recognition and having its own homeland." Further a confidential survey conducted by the central government of Pakistan quoted by the daily *News* some years back revealed that broadcasts of Urdu service of All India Radio were heard in 90 per cent homes in Karachi. Asked why they were switching to the enemy radio, some of the listeners replied that "this is the only source of correct pronunciation of Urdu for their family members, especially children."

Such assertions are being regarded by the compatriots of the Muhajirs as disloyalty and even treason. As alienation of

Muhajirs from other nationalities increased, their plight worsened. India should not remain unconcerned about their plight, not only from humanitarian angle but also because they are the largest NRI settled abroad.

The experience of the Urdu-speaking Muslims in the third country of the sub-continent viz India is hardly happier. The first and foremost casualty was of Urdu language which was dislodged from the status of dominant language of culture and politics in its homeland. They were the main targets of the riots in places outside their own region like Bhiwandi where they had migrated. Even in case of Gujarat, the epicenter of the communal trouble was in the U.P. The basic problems of the community in India is similar to that in Bangladesh and Pakistan viz of its urge for identity and of its adjustment with the requirements of other communities and of the national identity. But there is a vital difference. In India, the community is asserting its religious identity while in other countries of the sub-continent, it is asserting its cultural identity. Muslims like any other human beings need and belong to a multiplicity of identities; out of which religion and language are the most important basis of identity formation in the politics of the sub-continent. That identity becomes pronounced at a time which the people perceive to be threatened.

Siege mentality

As long as the Urdu-speaking Muslims suffer from a siege mentality, they would not be able to grow in all dimensions and unfold their cultural potentialities. But converse is also true. If their cultural potentialities are unfolded, it would be easier for them to get adjusted with other communities and feel free from the siege.

While it is important to discuss the role and obligations of Muslim identity in a secular India, it is equally important to know the needs and urges of the components of its identity and its cultural and ethnic dimensions. In fact a view from the sub-regional angle may be further instructive; to rediscover and replenish grass root level integrating forces e.g. folk tradition, legends, local faqirs and saints and even innocent superstitions. Some institutional innovations might be needed to strengthen such grass root forces. It is certainly not easy to remove all accumulated prejudices, fears and suspicions between the two major communities of India to resolve all contentious issues like the dispute in Ayodhya. But a beginning may be made with another approach at another level, besides what is being customarily done.

Taking note of the current deep psychological and political crisis of the Urdu-speaking Muslims in the changed sub-continental perspective, their indegenisational compulsions, and potential of a pluralist democratic polity, a fresh agenda may be drafted for an inter-community dialogue at micro-regional level. Much certainly needs to be done by this vital segment of the Muslim community in learning from lessons of the last over half a century, if not more, for properly analyzing its national and sub-continental dilemma and redefining its role and identity in an idiom that is understood and appreciated by others and in a manner that revives its creative potentialities. Similarly, Hindus, too, need to outgrow their obsessions about a simplistic view of a monolithic and transnational character of Islam and its extra-territorial loyalties and update their understanding of the ethnic, cultural and regional aspirations of the core of the Indian Muslims community.

In particular, three vital facts about the Urdu-speaking Muslims must be noted. Firstly, there is now no other Muslim society in the world which is intellectually and culturally superior to them and thus able to be a source of inspiration and loyalty to them. Pakistan has, in any case, lost that status. Secondly, their cultural roots lie deep within India and they are as much in need of continued cultural nourishment as any other people are. Thirdly, Urdu speaking Muslim community could possibly be the most vital bridge between India and Pakistan. In the interest of friendly relations between the two countries, this bridge needs to be strengthened.As major beneficiaries of the Samjhauta Express and peace process between India and Pakistan, their role becomes crucial in continuing them.

Such factors should also encourage an attempt, to arrest the present drift and correct an aberration in the behaviour of the

Ganga-Jamuna delta, the original home of the Urdu speaking Muslims of the subcontinent, that had deflected the course of the great Indian civilization six decades ago.

(*Economic and Political Weekly*, March 24-30, 2007, Vol. XLIII, No.12)

9

Muslim Personal Law: Uniformity Vs Reform

The celebrated Shah Bano case, had triggered almost polarised debate on the Muslim Personal Law, which had a major impact on community relations in independent India. Quoting the views of the leading members of the two communities and those of the English and Urdu press, the late Iqbal Masud, in a lengthy article in the *Indian Express*, found hardly any thing common between two solid blocs of opinions. However, the concluding para of the article was as follows: "Is the situation hopeless? No if you read writings of a person like Balraj Puri. Muslims will be well advised to interact with him."

I had never met Iqbal Masud before I read this reference to me. But it encouraged me to continue my interaction with the intellectuals of the two communities in seminars at various places where I did get a positive response. I used to make two main points. I was opposed to uniformity of personal laws but favoured need for reform in the Muslim Person Law.

Late Mirwaiz Maulvi Mohammad Farooq who had hosted a meeting of the All India Muslim Personal Law Board in Srinagar showed me his welcome address. He had argued that the Shariat law had divine sanction which no power on earth could change. It did not take me long to convince him that the law was not immutable. Thereupon he agreed to destroy the copies of his address and rewrite a new address on the lines I had suggested. Though, I admit that my role during that controversy had only a marginal impact, let me recall the respective arguments on both sides of the divide and my own comments on them.

There is perhaps no other issue on which Hindu community is more united than on the issue of a uniform personal law. From fanatic communal Hindus to secular and liberal Hindus, belonging to all ideological shades, all are unanimous on the subject. Their motives and arguments, of course, vary. Some want the 'privileged' position of Muslims to end. Some fear polygamy would upset the demographic balance. Some want uniformity for the sake of national integration. Some are motivated by sympathy for the Muslim women. The result is that the campaign for uniformity is being orchestrated from various forums — politics, press, academic centres, women organisations and judiciary.

Muslim opinion is similarly united in opposition to a uniform law, though it is comparatively less monolithic. Again, the arguments and motives vary. Their views range from opposition to uniformity to opposition to any change in the present Shariat Law. However, there is as little dialogue within the community as between it and other communities.

The first step towards restoration of a dialogue is to delink the two issues of uniformity and reform which need not have been linked and debate them separately on their respective merits.

The issue of personal law is, in fact, closely linked with the Muslim urge for identity. The near unanimity among the Muslims of the country against a uniform personal law is more a reflection of this urge than of their obscurantism. Similarly, most of the clamour for a common law by the Hindus is motivated by a desire for cultural and political uniformity rather than for reform of the so-called retrograde features of the Muslim law. In fact these features are usually cited merely to buttress the case for a common law.

Urge for Muslim Identity

The urge for identity of Muslims has survived their traumatic experience of the partition of India. Though the Muslim community, nationally and internationally, has its own peculiarities, its urge for identity is no different from the universal phenomenon of sharpening of ethnic and religious identities under the impact of modernisation.

Every identity has its symbols which are not acquired through a rational and conscious choice of its members but emerge imperceptibly through a complex interplay of factors.

The sudden fall of Urdu from the high cultural and political pedestal — though for known reasons —, changes in the Muslim character of Aligarh Muslim University and campaign for a uniform personal law threw up three rallying points for the Muslim community of India.

It does not mean that the Muslims today are in greater need for Urdu than English and the regional languages or that despite the mushroom growth of universities they still depend on Aligarh for their academic needs or that they are over-eager to marry four wives. The Muslim attitude on these issues is determined by entirely different reasons which need to be understood rather than merely condemned.

Nobody explicitly insists that subnational identities, including that of Muslims, should just cease to exist altogether. In a democratic and secular country, there is hardly any way of getting rid of them. What is in effect subject to debate is the legitimate limits and fields of the autonomy of these identities. It is argued, on the one side, that appeasement widens the limits of autonomy till it threatens national unity. But does not imposed uniformity provoke revolts of diversities and the resultant tension poses a greater threat to unity? On the other hand, a legitimate degree of autonomy, by providing means of gratification of sub-national urges, is likely to improve their emotional attachment with the nation and hence their sense of Indian patriotism and pride as Indian nationals.

Of course, autonomous rights must not transgress similar rights of other communities and override claims of national interest and commonly accepted national values.

Test Case

Muslim personal law has, in this context, in a way, become the test case. Whether it comes within the legitimate range and region of autonomy of Muslims is a question, on which opinion is sharply divided on communal lines. One vital question that arises in this connection is whether this autonomy is compatible with the principle of equality before law?

There is no doubt that in a secular democratic country all people likely to be involved in any action should be governed by the same law. If a Muslim robs or assaults a Hindu, or vice-versa, the criminal must be dealt with under the same law, irrespective of his community. Similarly, disputes over contracts, business deals, wages, employment, etc must be subject to uniform laws whatever be the caste, community and creed of the persons involved. For these logical reasons, codification of common criminal and civil laws by the British government was held by the 'ulama' of India to be in accordance with the spirit of the *shari'at*.

While communal diversity is not taken into account in criminal and civil legislation of the country, customary practice of various cultural groups are not completely disregarded. Variations of laws within other federations of the world are indeed wider. In USA for instance, not only criminal and civil laws vary from state to state, but even personal law, except that relating to monogamy, varies. The basic principle, however, is that people similarly situated, geographically, culturally, etc should be treated equally before law.

In India, as in any other federal country, legislative powers are shared by the Centre and the States. The latter have power to make laws on 66 entries on the state list and 47 entries on the concurrent list. These laws vary from state to state.

If diversity of these laws — based on geographical and cultural diversities — has not threatened the unity of the country

— would it be threatened if laws vary in accordance with religious diversities?

Variations in law to make allowance for variations in situations and categories of people are nothing unusual. What is usually resented is not the difference but the discrimination in treatment, unless it be in the nature of compensatory discrimination, i.e. conferring more than equal rights on the weaker sections.

Is the right of a Muslim male to marry four wives a discrimination against males of other communities? If at all it is a privilege, it is at the cost of Muslim women. And if the so called male privilege and female disprivilege are added up, can we surely say that the Muslim community is a privileged community on this account?

A graver apprehension, widely whispered and occasionally publicly expressed by many Hindus, is that Muslims insist on their legal right to polygamy — the only known provision of the Muslim personal law — with a view to outnumbering Hindus.

The first premise of the apprehension that legal provision for polygamy automatically leads to its practice is not substantiated by statistical studies. For the percentage of polygamous Muslim families is no larger than that of such families in any other community.

According to 1974 report of the National Commission on Women polygamy is more prevalent among non-Muslims than Muslims.

The second premise that polygamy would increase the total number of Muslim wives is logically fallacious. For if some men marry more than one woman, less women would be available for the remaining men, some of whom might have to remain unmarried. While the total stock of child bearing women would remain constant, the number of men engaged in the task of procreation would be reduced. Thus if at all polygamy makes a difference as compared to monogamy on the rate of population growth, it is likely to be in the direction of depressing it. For four men with four wives have chances of producing more children than one man with four wives.

Incidentally, the number of wives a Muslim may have under the present law is not limited to four. The law states, "if he marries a fifth wife, when he has already four, the marriage is not void (Batil), but merely irregular (Fasid)" (vide Mulla's "Mohammedan Law", section 255).

Liberal Argument

A sizeable liberal Hindu opinion is, in fact, outraged by such provisions of the Muslim law. While general opposition of Hindus to a separate personal law for Muslims is based on ignorance, prejudice or fear, liberals object to it on two grounds. First, the individual and not the community should be the basic unit of democracy. Second, Muslims too must benefit by a progressive law to the extent Hindus are doing.

The first is a question of should and reality. Shouldn't a liberal take cognizance of reality instead of imposing on it his view of it. Moreover, a community is also a means of self-expression of an individual.

The second argument confuses the issues of uniformity with reform. The solid resistance of the Muslim community to the question of reform of its personal law has been built up because it was linked with uniformity. No progress in the field of reform seems possible unless the two issues are delinked. Further, it is patronising to suggest that Muslim law should be as progressive as Hindu law. Why should not it be more or less than the latter in some of its provisions, depending in what one means by the adjective progressive?

Already in one crucial sense Muslim law is closer to the modern spirit. It is basically a contract between man and woman and not a sacrament as is the case in most other religions. It also implies that consent of the girl for marriage is necessary which nobody else — parent or guardian — can give on her behalf.

And what would one say of the Muta' (temporary) marriage, which the Shi'ah law recognises and in which the period of cohabitation is fixed and may be a term of years. In theory it could be as temporary as a year, a month, a day or a night.

A debate on what personal laws are progressive or desirable for the Muslim community is likely to be less inhibited if a uniform code is not insisted on. However, the case for reform in the Muslim personal law is as strong as the case for uniformity is weak.

Islamic Laws Not Rigid

Neither Muslim history nor any theological doctrine suggests that Islamic laws have been immutable and rigid.

The present Muslim personal law in India is a product of a long evolution and was subjected to many amendments. In its final form it was passed in 1937. There is no particular sanctity about this form or date. This law itself is based on Hanafi law which is one of the many schools of Islamic jurispudence. These schools are not divine revelations as such but are the products of a long debate and study by the great scholars of Islam. Their works are, of course, based on the *Qur'an, Hadith, Qiyas* and *Ijma*. But the very fact that there were more than one school of jurispudence and were evolved at different point of time and space, clearly implies that none of them can claim finality for all times to come.

As M. Hidayatullah observes in his introduction to "Principles of Mohamedan Law" (Bombay, 1969), "the invocation of the right of the Ruler (or the State) to take public good into account, to change an established rule, is not new. It was practised by the Khulafai-Rashidin. Changes in Hadd (limit of punishment) were made from time to time as a part of public policy, during the Prophet's own time and that of all the Caliphs. Citing an instance, Hidayatullah says that while the Prophet did not order compensation against a bailee who had lost the bailed article by theft, without any neglect on his part, Caliph Umar ordered such compensation because the bailees began to take advantage of the rule.

Again the governor designate of Yaman, according to a Hadith, told the Prophet that he would use his own reason in making decisions on issues on which he failed to get guidance from the holy book or the usage of the Prophet. The Prophet approved of it which is an eloquent testimony to the fact that Islam is not unresponsive to new situations not contemplated in the *Qur'an* and the *Hadith*.

During the 1400 year long odyssey of Islam through a large part of the world, Islamic laws are known to have widely changed, from time to time and country to country. Even within India, all Muslim communities in different parts do not follow a uniform personal law and the courts respect diversities of customs and practices. The acceptance of modern common criminal and civil laws without any reservations by the Muslim intelligentia and masses in India — as also in many other countries of the world including Muslim countries — in place of what was strictly ordained in the Qur'an again bears out the fact that Islam has been responding to the needs of the times. However, Islamic scholars have insisted that all reforms must be subject to the fundamental moral and spiritual principles of Islam.

Real controversy is, however, not about the possibility and need of change in laws but its manner; who has the authority to decide that fundamental principles have not been violated?

There are four known sources of Islamic law and hence of reform: the *Qur'an, Hadith, Qiyas* and *Ijma*. While divine revelation through the *Qur'an* and the practices and precedents of the Prophet recorded in the Hadith are the final authority. Qiyas or interpretation of their intention must guide in situations uncovered by them.

It is, however, the concept of Ijma, the consensus of the opinion of scholars, which has the power of independent judgement or innovation called Ijtihad; that is a distinctive feature of the rationality of Islam.

Spirit of Ijtihad

Many Muslim scholars have urged the revival of the spirit of Ijtihad to restore a dynamic role to Islamic jurisprudence. Ameer

Ali (1849-1928) who made a pioneering contribution to reviving Muslim consciousness in the subcontinent as an original thinker bewailed that "a follower of Muhammad should abandon his judgement completely to the interpretations of men who lived in the 9th century and could have no conception of the necessities of the 20th."

Similarly, Mohammad Iqbal (1876-1938) attached special importance to Ijtihad as a source of Muslim law. In his famous "Lectures on Reconstruction of Religious Thought in Islam" he held that Ijtihad "within the limits of the revealed text, is absolutely free" and "was permitted even in the life-time of Holy Prophet" (Delhi edition, p. 147)

With the expansion of the sphere of Islam, territorially and numerically, it became increasingly difficult to hold an Ijma. For Islam is not a cadre-based, hierarchised church with registered ulama. Who is then authorised to convene an Ijma? What should be the qualifications of the participants? Should they merely be scholars of Arabic and theology or also of modern knowledge? But who is to determine religious and secular qualifications?

As Iqbal gives serious thought to the questions of Ijtihad and Ijma, his learned views deserve to be quoted at length to form the starting point of a discussion on the subject.

He believes that principle of change applies even to eternal principles. For "change is, according to the Qur'an, one of the greatest signs of God." He, therefore, regrets the immobility of Islam for the last 500 years largely due to the decline in the spirit of Ijtihad (p. 147).

Iqbal does not regard the Qur'an as a legal code (p 165). Treating it as a source of moral and spiritual guidance, he relies on Sura 26:69' "Those who exert themselves in our paths, we will surely guide." He rejects the claim of the 'Ulama' of Islam about the finality of the Mohammedan law and pleads for Ijtihad to reinterpret it in "the light of modern experience and the altered conditions of the modern life." (p. 168)

Faced with the problems of convening an Ijma, Iqbal observes: "Legislative assembly is the only possible form Ijma could take in modern times", to which the power of Ijtihad may be transferred. In other words, laws passed by Parliament would be as valid as those adopted by Ijma of earlier times. If the Muslim personal law was passed by a majority of Muslim MPs while others abstained, the decision, according to Iqbal's logic, should have perfect religious sanctity.

While there may be no unanimity about the modus operandi, scholarly opinion overwhelming favours the view that Muslims have a right to change their laws (i.e. those which exclusively concern them). In any case, who but Muslims can decide that they have this right.

Right of Women

It seems unlikely that the Muslim community can be led to believe that equality of sexes is in conflict with the spirit of Islam. But who is the final authority on the basic principle, the Constitution or the community? If the community, can its male members arrogate the right to decide that they have superior rights over females? Or shouldn't it be the right of Muslim women to decide whether they continue to prefer an inferior status? If the right of non-Muslims to impose their views on the legal status of the families of Muslims is challenged, the right of the Muslim men to impose their views on the status of women would similarly be challenged.

While Mohammedan law permits a Male Muslim to have as many as four wives (fifth marriage being irregular though not void) "it is not lawful for Mohomedan women to have more than one husband at the same time" (Mulla, Sections 255 and 256). The provisions for men and women in this respect are grossly different and inequitable.

As far as divorce is concerned, "any Mohamedan of sound mind, who has attained puberty, may divorce his wife whenever he desires without assigning any cause" (Mulla, Section 308). The divorce may be oral or written (Section 310).

The power to give divorce belongs primarily to the husband, But he has a right to delegate the power to his wife who by virtue of power acquired from her husband can divorce him (Mulla, Section 314). It, again, is a patently unequal position.

However, the Dissolution of Muslim Marriages Act VIII of 1939 gives substantial relief to Muslim woman on this issue and lays down the following grounds of divorce, (i) the whereabouts of the husband are unknown for a period of four years; (2) failure of the husband to provide for the maintenance of the wife for a period of two years; (3) sentence of imprisonment on husband for a period of seven years; (4) failure without reasonable cause to perform marital obligations; (5) impotence of husband; (6) insanity of husband; (7) repudiation of marriage by wife (a minor girl married by a father or grandfather has a right to repudiate marriage after attaining age of 18 years provided it was not consummated); (8) Cruelty of husband, and (9) apostasy from Islam of the husband.

The enactment definitely improved the status of Muslim women. But all the grounds for divorce in the case of a woman are subject to proof and judicial scrutiny whereas a man need not assign any reason for divorcing his wife. This is far from the requirements of equality of sexes.

Inequality is equally glaring in the law relating to guardianship. For it recognises the father as the primary and natural guardian of his minor children. The mother is only entitled to the custody of her male child until the age of seven and of her female child until she attains puberty. But the right of custody is subject to the supervision of the father and this right, too, lapses after her remarriage.

The law of inheritance is no less inequitable. For whatever be the line of succession, the share of male heirs at every level shall be twice that of female heirs at that level.

Some eminent Muslims do maintain that Mahomedan law does not represent the spirit of Islam. But the only way to judge the spirit of Islam is by the direction it gave to pre-Islamic laws and customs. The attempt to humanise an unjust patriarchal system was indeed revolutionary. It is unfair to measure the reforms introduced by Islam, torn out of its historical context, in terms of the values of today Equality of sexes is a very recent concept which is a product of opportunities of independent careers for women and universal education and franchise.

The traditional rights of a man were based on the presumption that he was the head of the family, its bread-winner and protector. (Qur'an 4:34). What would the spirit of the Qur'an indicate if this situation changes and woman is no more exclusively dependent on man? The situation may call for a revolutionary change in the status of women in society, as the Prophet had introduced in the Arabian society 1,400 years ago. Isn't it a solution like this for which Islam had made a provision of Ijtihad?

Uniformity vs. Integration

The purpose of this note is not to settle all legal and theological issues on the subject. It merely examines the scope for reform in Islamic laws, on human, constitutional and religious grounds and the capacity of the reformed laws to meet the needs of modern society. It is a plea for a debate on a subject of vital importance to Muslim community as it concerns the happiness of its families, the urge of its women for an equitable status and its socio-economic life. Such a debate should not only be possible but should also become necessary if it is insulated against the threats and provocations of a uniform personal code. In fact the debate itself would help in ensuring this insulation. Needless to add, the health and growth of a community also depend on its ability to debate its problems. And no tradition has survived long without continuously changing.

Some sort of debate is, in fact, going on in the Muslim community. It has, for instance, been vigorously pleaded that a permissible and not a compulsory law may be enacted for those who may opt for it. Again, the All India Women Conference, under the presidentship of Begum Hamid Ali, had suggested way back in the early thirties the inclusion of the rights of women in the

Nikahnamah. As Muslim marriage is based on the principle of contract, it can be made as equitable as one likes without violating the present law and a rigid fundamentalist position. Kamila Tyabji who has been campaigning for this course and whose family has been following it, refers, in this context, to an agreement drafted by a Muslim firm of solicitors included as an appendix in Fyzee's "Outlines of the Mohamadan Law" as also to a "shorter and much dramatic version of the contract" drafted by Daniel Latifi which bears the stamp of the Chief Qazi of Aligarh. The latter had three provisions: first, equal position of husband and wife as regards divorce, second *mehr*, half of which to be paid immediately and the rest deferred to death or divorce; and third, no right of polygamy to the husband.

Akhtar Sultan Begum of Lucknow had provided an answer to the current controversy over the triple talaq that was triggered by the All-India Muslim Personal Law Board's (AIMPLB) recent decision which held it to be an evil but opposed any law against it.

The 88-year-old Begum had got a clause, granting her the right to divorce (tafviz-e-talaq) inserted in her nikahnama in 1936. Since then she has also ensured that every woman who got married in her family has used the same nikahnama. The Begum, however, never had to invoke that clause as she lived happily with her husband, Dr Ajmal Hassan Khan, till his death in 1985. But she set a precedent which can be used by any Muslim family, within the framework of the present Muslim Perssonal Law.

Rejection of triple talaq, though implied, could be provided more specifically. Another draft of nikahnama was submitted by a group of Muslim women a few years back to the AIMPLB but got no response.

The board has, at its last meeting in the first week of July, 2003, come out with a concrete suggestion "to promote a nikahnama which would provide for arbitration if differences arise between a couple." But why should the terms of contract of marriage he confined to merely drafts, including that of Danial Latiff or the one being used by the family of Akhtar Sultan or Kamila Tyabji, be called less authentic, legally or theologically? Or why should a single "model draft" be applicable to all families all the times? If some authority, however able and great scholars its members may be, assumed the right to impose terms of contract on the contracting parties, it ceases to be a contract that Islam had granted.

It is a liberal trend like this that is threatened with the obsession of the Hindus, including liberals, for uniformity of the civil law.

Finally, the role of judiciary in setting the clock of reform of Muslim Personal law back needs also be discussed. For it was not the judicial judgement of the Chief Justices of the Supreme Court of India as such that provoked strong reactions but their obiter dicta. They clearly trespassed into a domain about which their knowledge and authority could be challenged. They cited the cause of national integration that his judgement intended to serve. Judicial decisions should be based on legal merit and not on doubtful political considerations. Moreover, the actual effect of his judgement was a serious blow to the cause of national integration. The chain reaction that followed Shah Bano case will bear that out. For to neutralise sharp Muslim reaction, the Congress government got a hurriedly drafted Muslim Women (Protection of Rights on Divorce) Act passed in 1986; It caused Hindu backlash. The BJP tried to cash on it by incorporating Ayodhya issue on its agenda. To counteract it, the Congress government allowed the *Shilanayas* ceremony in the disrupted territory in Ayodhya. The chain of events that culminated in the demolition of the Babri Masjid clearly demonstrated that the issue of national integration is beyond the competence and jurisdiction of their lordship.

Another objectionable part of his obiter dicta was his audacity to quote Quranic verses in support of the judgement. For no court of law has the authority to interpret religious scriptures.

A decade after the Shah Bano case, Justice Kuldip Singh made similar observations in his obiter dicta. The high office he held did not qualify him to pronounce judgements on issues of "national unity and solidarity". By premising that Muslim Personal law cannot be reformed without making it a part of uniform law", the learned judge subordinated the cause of Muslim women to the Muslim urge for identity and thus did grave injustice to their cause.

He also pronounced that no community could claim to remain a separate entity on the basis of religion. The degree of autonomy of a religious, caste, linguistic and other entities is to be decided by political considerations in a federal democratic country. On a subject like this any political activist or a teacher of social sciences is better qualified than their lordships of the apex court.

Another prejudice that Justice Kuldip Singh fostered was that while "Hindus have forsaken their sentiments in the cause of national unity and integration, Muslims have not". It is totally incorrect statement. The Hindu code Bill has certainly done a lot of good to the Hindu community but by no stretch of imagination can it be related to the cause of national unity and integration. And how could Hindu Code Bill and its later amendments — which are exclusively applicable to Hindus be called uniform law? If a separate law was evolved in stages for Hindus in their own interest why a different yardstick is being insisted on for Muslims? Why cannot their law be reformed like the Hindu law in stages and in their own interest. It need not be as "progressive" — depending on the angle you view it — as the Hindu law. It could be, as pointed out earlier, more or less than that which should be decided by the community.

Justice Singh need not have laboured to trace political and legal history of the country to demonstrate how a common civil and criminal law was evolved. For, as discussed earlier, there is no dispute about that and cannot be equated with personal law as it does not affect any other community.

At a time when diversity and pluralism have been recognised as most celebrated values, voices of uniformity are being raised by short sighted politicians who, unfortunately draw support from the verdict of highest judiciary authority, in their non-judicial authority. Both do not realize the contradiction between unity and uniformity.

(Muslim India, January-July, 2003)

10

Religion in Indian Politics

If the way prolonged controversy over the relation between religion and politics in India is generating more heat than light, it is primarily on account of lack of clarity and agreement on the precise concept of religion as also politics.

When stalwarts of the freedom movement like Mahatma Gandhi, Maulana Azad, Khan Abdul Ghaffar Khan and Sheikh Abdullah, who laid the basis of Indian secularism, insisted on drawing their inspiration for their politics from religion they had a concept of religion which was different from, say, those who organized separate political party for their religious community and demanded a separate homeland for it.

Those who argue that religion and politics should not be mixed up, Gandhi had said, do not know what religion is.

It may also be recalled that Sheikh Abdullah fought his decisive battles against the Muslim League and its slogan of Pakistan from the mosques and shrines of Kashmir. And the anti-British Sikh movement, also an ally of the national movement, was based in gurdwaras. Both these movements were hailed as secular by the nationalists leadership.

Further many secularists maintain that religion should be nothing more than a matter between man and his maker and its proper place is either the solitude of the house or the church betray an inadequate understanding of what constitutes a religion. Apart trom a mode of worship, religion is also a set of ideas and values. In this role, religion is a source of inspiration and moral discipline for many of its followers. It is neither possible nor justified to deprive them of this source.

One need not be a believer in religion much less in what is called communalism to know that it does not consist merely in prayer to God but also covers set of theological beliefs, rituals and practices which one shares with the community. More than anything, religion is a cultural and social entity. Indeed, it is inconceivable without a community.

Mode of prayer, concept of God and other religious and spiritual doctrines are rarely the main source of tension between communities these days. When religious communities fight, usually they do so on secular demands e.g. share in the economic cake, government jobs, admissions to technical institutions and, above all, political power.

Likewise politics as an activity for pursuit of power is different from urge for identity of various religious and other groups.

Religion is also a system of theological beliefs and dogmas. In this role it may be deficient in rational contents and many a rationalist may condemn it as obscurantist. In the West much blood was shed on account of theological differences. But not a single communal conflict in India can be traced to such differences. The conflict here is more due to communal than religious causes. Even the dispute in Ayodhya, which led to worst bloodshed in the country since independence, did not relate to any religious issue but to claims over real estate. At no stage any Muslim showed disrespect to Ram. Nor even the most fanatic Hindu challenged the right of Muslims to build mosques, except at the disputed site. Even in Gujarat program, no theological differences were ever mentioned. There were hints about loyalty of Muslims and their sympathy for Pakistan.

This brings us to the third role of religion i.e. as a social community. It is a vital basis of identity formation. Even those who do not share its theological beliefs or follow its rituals and are agnostic or atheists form part of the community by virtue of their family and social ties.

It is this role of religion which poses a problem in politics. For most of the religious communities are tending to acquire socio-political aspirations. Development, mobility, media and information explosion, politicization and adult franchise are further encouraging a sense of self-awareness among the people. As class, political and ideological identities have not grown fast enough, religious identities filled that vacuum. Even in the United States, as Robert Booth Fowler observes, religion is becoming an answer to "continuing yearning for a community." It provides " sense of certainty and community within the larger society's uncertainty and impersonality."

Further as the system in India is extremely inadequate to recognize individual identities and to provide security and justice to them, many people seek them through their communal identity. Thus community is as important an entity in politics as an individual. Under these circumstances, no secular system can be built in India by dismissing altogether the reality of communal identities and their claims in economic and political fields. For instance, a cabinet in any State or at the Centre which is composed of a single community, caste or region will not be acceptable to others on the plea that merit of its individual members was the exclusive criterion.

The real question is not whether politics should recognize identities. How can politics-which is called an art of the possible-ignore realities? But the question that needs to be debated and has not been properly debated is what is the legitimate field of these identities and the degree of their autonomy.

How these identities are to be related to one another, to other forms of identities and to the national identity? Or, in other words, the question is not whether religion and politics are related to each other but what should be the precise nature of their relationship.

The debate on the subject has been much influenced by the European experience which is not entirely relevant to India. Firstly, unlike the countries of Europe, India is not a uni-religious country. Secondly, Europe has a history of domination of Pope over the State and even now Christian political parties exist in many parts of it.

India's own past is far more relevant in this context. For, unlike Europe, India does not have a history of a theocratic state. As far as Hindus are concerned, there is no treatise on politics that is regarded by them as an infallible or divine scripture. In fact, the tradition of Raja and Rishi represents a clear distinction between a spiritual and temporal role. The two roles were inter-connected but autonomous.

Eight hundred years of rule by the Muslim Kings in India is equally marked by its pluralistic character. Though the king and the ulama interacted, secular authority always reigned supreme. A third dimension of the Muslim polity, viz. Sufis, carved out their own autonomous domain, often in defiance of both the king and the ulama.

The lesson of the Sikh history is no different. The fact that spiritual and temporal affairs were conceptualized in the Sikh tradition by Guru Hargobind Singh by the two swords that he kept, symbolising peeri and meeri (spiritual and temporal) respectively, and two separate fora of Harminder Sahib and Akal Takhat clearly implied duality, Sikh religion and politics, though closely related, were autonomous. The autonomous character of their leadership and institutions became more pronounced after the gurus. The greatest Sikh prince Ranjit Singh, for instance, never claimed any religious authority nor any religious leader aspired for political power. Muslims and Hindus occupies highest positions in his government.

Any attempt to project a monolithic religious and political identity of a community, would, thus, not only be a negation of the entire history of religious communities in India but would also retard its future growth. Those who claim that religion and politics are inseparable to the extent that all members of a religious community should belong to a single political party imply subordination of religion to politics. To seek unity of a community on the basis of complete political agreement means loss of political freedom to its members. Such unity can only be attempted by regimentation and arousing a sense of hatred of the community against another to a hysterical pitch, which in no way promotes its mental health.

In practice, such subordination of religion to politics not only devalues the former but, in an open society and under normal conditions, is the surest way of disintegration of a community. For political ambitions of its leaders are bound to clash. And political differences are bound to exist in a free society.

There is another serious implication of organizing political parties exclusively on the basis of religious communities. If all voters remain faithful to their respective religious parties, the system of election would become redundant and political balance would be frozen to the numerical strength of various communities. This would lead to permanent political majority and minority which, in other words, would mean permanent domination of the former over the latter. As the individual members of the former too would not have any option it would amount to their regimentation and a good bye to democracy.

Thus complete merger of institutionalized religion and institutionalized politics into a monolithic forum would create as anomalous a situation as their complete separation. In practice, members of every community need to associate with those of other communities to promote their class, professional and cultural interests through, say, organizations of workers, peasants, occupational groups, writers, artists, etc. So far no religious leader has objected to autonomy of such organisations from religion. Why should not it apply to politics in the interest of intellectual freedom of the members of the community and of a more abiding basis of its unity? These fields can neither be put into watertight compartments nor merged into a single monolithic entity without emasculating them.

In sum, instead of posing the question in either or terms, a more fruitful line of approach would be to debate appropriate relationship between religion, in both ideological and institutional forms, and politics and define the spheres of their autonomy. In this task, India's own historical experience and contemporary realities cannot be ignored.

(The Radical Humanist, Vol. 57, No. 2, May 1993)

11

Mythology of Muslim Politics in India

Muslims in Free India by Moin Shakir; Kalamkar Prakashan, New Delhi; pp 156; Rs. 20

"The days of religion-oriented politics are over", fondly asserts Moin Shakir in the beginning of the book under review. "The vigour of the so-called two nations theory and the idea of the economic emancipation of the Muslims from the Hindus has gone", he adds.

Having said this, he proceeds to refute the view in the rest of his book. He believes that Muslims, who have neither wealth nor position, are economically worse than Hindus. They are thus "frustrated, demoralized, pessimistic and confused". He lists more grievances of the Muslims which sustain their communal consciousness. All Muslim organizations, according to him, are separatists. Generalising about the Muslim mind, the author further makes the following observations: "Islam is the dominant theoretical pattern which proliferates into all the basic activities of the Indian Muslims... The Indian Muslims have chosen to be the inheritors of the orthodox legacy of Sheikh Ahmed Sirhindi and Shah Waliullah... Muslims are opposed to joint electorate... communalism had been the political ideology of the Muslim elite... which ... was prone to assume the form of popular ideology."

These generalizations about the conditions and attitudes of the Muslims are no less sweeping than the statement that "days of religion-oriented politics are over". For, like any other religious community, there is a diversity of views and status - economic, political and social - among the Muslims also. The author himself attests that "the Muslim community is not as homogenous, well-knit and consolidated as its leaders wish us to believe."

There is a similar simplification in the author's description of the Hindu mind. For a detailed discussion of Hindu nationalism, he depends mainly on AAK Soze's interpretation, published in Jamait-I-Islami's organ *Radiance*, instead of that of any spokesman of Hindus or communal Hindus.

In any case, the entire analysis of the book - however exaggerated and oversimplified - contradicts the author's view that the days of religion-oriented politics are over. He even argues that, after 1947, "there has been a tendency to justify consolidation of the communities along religious lines." And he is alarmed by the fact that "the secular elements are being rendered ineffective."

But he finds a ray of hope in the voting behaviour of the Muslims which, according to him, indicates that they are getting disillusioned with the traditional elite leadership. D.R. Goyal reinforces this conclusion in the introduction to the book. If voting behaviour is any guide, he argues, the Muslims, on the whole, have never listened to them (i.e. the communal leaders).

Shakir and Goyal have jumped to far-off conclusions from insufficient grounds. That the Muslims had, by and large, been voting for the Congress was, in itself, not conclusive proof of the non-existence of Muslim communalism. The voter has to choose between available alternatives. If the main challenge to the Congress is from a party like the Jan Sangh — as used to be the case in most of northern India - it is natural for a communal Muslim to vote for the former as the lesser evil. In similar circumstances, Hindu voters of the Punjab had often preferred the Congress to the Akali Dal. But it does not prove that the communal politics has no hold on the Hindus of that state.

Voting behaviour would be a truer indicator of the Muslim mind in those areas where the main contest is between a Muslim party and the Congress or any other secular party, so that splitting of Muslim votes does not help a Hindu communal party. The fact that more candidates are returned by the Muslim League in the southern states than by the Muslim parties of the northern states does not prove that the South is more communal than the North. The point need not be laboured further, as the author himself concedes that the Muslim community, since 1952, has voted for the Congress on communal grounds.

Moin Shakir has no sympathy with communalism. Perhaps he resorts to oversimplifications in his analysis to cover up the discrepancy between the reality and his wishes.

Occasionally, however, the author does show promise of bold analysis. His characterization of the so-called nationalist and communal Muslims, for instance, stands in refreshing contrast to the standard official view. In his present volume and the predecessor volume - "*Khilafat to Partition*" - he exposes the obscuranist and orthodox character of the nationalist Muslims while showing an appreciation of the modern outlook of some of the Muslim leaders who had opted out of the nationalist movement. It is good to be reminded that Sir Syed Ahmed Khan, Dr Mohammad Iqbal, and Mohammad Ali Jinnah took an enlightened view of Islam and opposed its narrow and orthodox interpretations.

In this respect Moin Shakir's work is as valuable as that of Aziz Ahmad ("*Islamic Modernism in India and Paksitan*", London, 1967). But Ahmed is far more consistent in linking the movement of Islamic modernism with that of Pakistan and the post-Partition leadership of the new country. Shakir, on the other hand, is modernist as well as a nationalist Indian. He has not been able to reconcile the modernism and the separatism of some of the Muslim leaders.

He regards Sir Syed as the greatest liberal among the Muslim thinkers in India ("*Khilafat to Partition*"). He traces secular trends in contemporary Muslim to him. (*Secular Democracy*, Annual 1969).

He finds the remedy to communalism in a process of modernization, of which Sir Syed was the pioneer ("*Muslims in Free India*").

But the author contradicts this assessment of Sir Syed when he admits that "the logical end of his political programme was isolationism, separatism, withdrawal and adherence to mendicancy". He quotes Halide Edile ("*Inside India*") to say that Aligarh produced men "mostly fanatical and stagnant in mind" (*"Khilafat to Partition*"). He also admits that Aligarh played a vital role in the growth of Musilm nationalism, which resulted in the partition of the country, and that "it was practically converted into an intellectual rendezvous to the Muslim League" (*Muslims in Free India*). Incidentally, there is a discrepancy in the two works of the author on a minor issue of Sir Syed's view on pardah. In the book under review, he states that Sir Syed - along with others - "voiced strong protest against the system of pardah". But in his earlier book ("*Khilafat to Partition*"), he believed that Sir Syed was not progressive in his social views because "he supported the system of pardah."

Moin Shakir discards one myth to fall prey to another. Just as anti-British attitudes and support of national independence are not necessarily the acid tests of progressivism and secularism, so modernism too is not synonymous with secularism. The author seems to share AB Shah's enthusiasm for modernization of Indian Muslims as a pre-condition to their 'decommunalisation'.

Communalism, believes the author, demands a traditionalist social structure for effective functioning. This is simply not true. The leadership and the ranks of the Muslim League were in no sense more traditionalist than the Muslim supporters of the Congress. It was no accident that Aligarh, and not Deoband, became he rendezvous of the Muslim League. Again, modernised industrial townships, like Jamshedpur, Ranchi and Ahmedabad, have been more prone to communal riots than the traditional towns and the countryside.

Nor is Hindu communalism based on traditionalist social structure. The Arya Samaj movement, which sought to reinterpret Hinduism in a modern idiom, gave the initial militancy to the community. In the present times, it is the middle-class urban population which comprised the backbone of a party like the Jan Sangh (predecssor of the BJP). In states like Maharashtra, Andhra and Mysore, where the party has no mass base, it often succeed in getting its candidates elected from graduate and teacher constituencies of the legislature or the university.

The author refuses to face the fact (because it is unpleasant?) That communalism, as we understand the term, is a by-product of modernization. According to his thinking, it is the urge for a political entity on the part of a community that is appropriately called communalism. Such an urge is obviously a modern phenomenon. Development of communications and education creates among people a consciousness of the geographical and historical continuity of a community. Muslim communalism, as the author rightly observes, should be considered a part of the mobilization and politicisation process - hence, one may add, of the process of modernization.

Communalism is, after all, concerned with secular, i.e. non-religious demands of a community, such as its representation in services, politicals and educational institutions. These demands are more intensely felt by the educated and modernized than by the traditionalist sections of the society.

The author exaggerates the influence of the Ulama who, according to an authority quoted by him, "have direct contact with the masses and are able to guide their attitudes and opinions." Jinnah's influence on Indian Muslims, Sheikh Abdullah's on Kashmiri Muslims, and ZA Bhutto's on Pakistani Muslims, in defiance of the traditionally established Ulama, expose the myth of the hold of traditionalists on the Muslim masses.

The foregoing arguments do not imply a commendation of communalism or a condemnation of modernisation; just as to be conscious of the evils that normally follow in the wake of industrialization does not imply a plea against it.

The author tries to explain the nature of Muslim communalism from another angle. He lists grievances and problems of Muslims in two separate chapters, (What, incidentally, is the difference between grievances and problems?), which, according to him, sustain Muslim communal consciousness.

The degree of communal consciousness is not proportional to the amount of discontent among the members of a community. It is essentially a product of a commonly shared experiences - be this of satisfaction or dissatisfaction, achievement or failure. The problems that Muslims are faced with would contribute to their communal consciousness, only if they are due to their being Muslims and are articulated and redressed exclusively by the efforts of the leaders of the community.

The problem that should least contribute to communalism is the economic problem. Why should, for instance, poor Muslims be driven, merely on account of their poverty, to rally round rich Muslims instead of joining hands with the poor of the other communities? Unless appeal of communal solidarity is stronger - than the class appeal -economic causes do not promote communalism. The grievances and problems, however, act as the catalytic agents of rationalizations of communal consciousness.

What, then, is the basic cause? Is it the nature of Islam? Put in this blunt form, the author would reply in the negative. According to him, "it is only a particular interpretation put on it" that is responsible for the evil of communalism.

However, he finds that, according to his own assessment and interpretation also, Islam and Islamic heritage are responsible for an urge among Muslims to have distinctive entity which cannot be easily merged with the national identity. For Islam, he maintains, gives its followers a transnational view. The author further makes the following daring observations:

"The social system of Islam reflects feudal spirit... A religion which claims to be all-comprehensive and perfect for all times necessarily encourages reactionary politics and outdated political ideas... The superiority of Islamic ideology negates the concept of the unity of al religions. In a multi-religious society, it certainly comes in the way of the ideal of human equality, such a view of religion gives impetus to aggressive expansionism."

The observations are in keeping with the style of the author which is prone to simplistic generalizations. But, even if it were the whole truth about Islam, it does not explain every Muslim behaviour everywhere. Many Muslim communities are known to be intensely nationalist as also tolerant towards minorities.

The author quotes AB Shah's argument on the origin of the communal attitude of the Muslims. Wherever Muslims are in a minority, says Shah, they refuse to merge into the national mainstream and insist on maintaining a separatist posture. MRA Baig argues the same point as follows: "Islam, as generally practiced, developed its way of life and ethos in countries in which Muslims were in a majority. It was developed as a religion of Muslims, by Muslims, for Muslims. It did not envisage or legislate for Muslims in a minority. In consequence, there is no guidance, in either the Quran, by any hadith, or by the great Islamic jurists to Muslims on how to live as a minority in harmony with their fellow critizens in non-Muslim countries." (*Indian Express*, December 16, 1971)

In a way, all minorities tend to behave the same way. They are extrasensitive to the preservation of their identity. The so-called liberal community of the Hindus is likely to be responsive to communal politics in states such as Punjab and Kashmir where it is the minority.

Apart from the minority character and historical background of Muslim Indians, it is the peculiar character of Hinduism that influences their attitude. More than a creed or a set of practices, Hinduism is a geographical and racial entity. It is confined to India or people of Indian origin.

Unlike Muslims of most other lands, the Muslims in India do not pride in their pre-Islamic history, as - apart from other reasons - it lands them into the domain of another religion. Indianisation and Hinduisation go hand-in-hand a long way. For Indian nationalism and Hinduism are essential constituents of each other. What we call Hindu communalism, is essentially an extreme form of nationalism which is intolerant towards the supposedly less loyal elements in the society.

The author repeats the well-worn cliché of the secularists that communalism of one community is the sustainer of the communalism in another. It is, however, factually incorrect to say that Muslim communalism is a mere reaction to Hindu communalism. For, Jinnah reacted to Gandhi - the authentic voice of Hindus - and not to Golwalkar, who was a comparatively far more obscure person at that time.

The author quite rightly views communalism "as a consequence of the contradictions of Indian nationalism". The concept of Indian nationalism is still inadequate, and its capacity to inspire various communities of the country is not uniform.

He also rightly quotes WC Smith to say that the 'Indian Muslim is both Indian and Muslim' and adds "Indianness and Muslimness are equally valid and interdependent." But would it not be more correct to say that the Indianness of a Muslim is still subcontinentalist? For, Muslim Indians have not cut their umbilical chord from the sub continental Muslim identity. In fact, the pronounced form of what is called transnationalism of Muslim Indians is also subconentalism.

The truth is that neither all Muslims nor all Hindus are fully reconciled to the partition of the country. But what really offends the majority community is that the centre of transnational affinities of the Muslim Indian should tend to be around Islamabad. (For a full discussion of the problem of sub continental identity of the Muslim Indian, see 'Restructuring the Subcontinent' by Balraj Puri. (*Economic, and Political Weekly*, Annual Number 1972). Moin Shakir gives due recognition to the Muslim urge for identity. But he does not seem to be much conscious of its sub continental dimension.

Again, there is a subtle but vital difference between the problem of Muslim identity and of the identity of Muslims. What are the identities - apart from the Muslim identity - which can provide a sense of belonging to individual Muslims? No single identity can represent a full personality. For his proper growth and satisfaction, every individual needs to belong to a plurality of identities, which by cutting across one another avoid exclusiveness and link each individual with every other. Religion, region, language, class, profession, ideology and party seem to divide. But each is not only a source of cohesion for its adherents; if none claims exclusive loyalty, each also neutralizes the divisive aspects of the other. Multiplicity of mutually balanced intermediary identities is thus the surest method of integrating a multitude of individuals into nationhood.

But Moin Shakir sees Indian reality in a simpler form. For him integration merely implies "breaking up of the communal identities and the consequent emergence of the Indian identity." In reality, there are - and should be - more than two forms of identities. Moreover, Indian identity cannot be created out of a vacuum, following the break-up of communal identities. It must grow out of a process of synthesis and reconciliation between numerous smaller identities.

What role should religion-based identity have in such a pluralistic set up? The author draws a distinction between two aspects of this identity - political and socio-cultural. While he concedes that 'it is legitimate on the part of the minority to maintain and preserve its social and cultural uniqueness', he is opposed to political organizations on communal lines.

This is a sound distinction, but it should not be accepted without serious qualifications. Short of a separate political organization for each community, other conventions and arrangements have to be devised to ensure an equitable share in political power to all communities. In this sense, secular politics must not fail to take cognizance of communal identities.

While underplaying the role of communal identities in politics, the author overplays their socio-cultural role. For, there are a few social and cultural fields which can be exclusively identified with a communal identity. What, for instance, is meant by a unique and separate social entity of Muslims? Does it mean that clubs, sports, and entertainments, should also be organized on a communal basis? And what is Muslim culture? Have language, literature, art and music a religion? Is not culture of, say, a Bengali Muslim closer to that of a Hindu Bengali than to that of a Punjabi Muslim? In fact, emotionally viable non-communal identities can more easily grow in social and cultural fields than in politics. Such identities alone can provide a secure basis for secular politics.

A mentally grown-up Muslim must be a proud Muslim, a proud, say, Kashmiri, a proud Indian, and may proudly belong to organizations representing his/her political views, business or class interests, literary and cultural urge, social attachments and religious needs. S/he may legitimately have an urge to belong to transnational identities; ideological, professional and even religious. It must be convenient to divide his/her sense of belonging into political and non-political. But, in both fields, he/she could share a common sense of belonging with some non-Muslims also. And, in many political as well as non political fields, he/she might still be identified as a member of his/her community. Suitable institutional arrangements and conventions can be devised to provide a sense of belonging and also a sense of identity to the Muslims of India.

This is a field into which Moin Shakir does not venture. His main job is to assess and interpret the existing Muslim political thought in the country, and not to extend it. But, even that job requires a proper conceptual framework which Muslim studies in India have not yet acquired.

Indian Muslim studies are no more a neglected subject. They have attracted a good deal of foreign scholarship also. But their grooves were set long ago. With a rational and enlightened mind, Moin Shakir offered a promise to bring in, as the blurb puts it, 'a whiff of fresh air'. But sharper analytical tools and a more rigorous mental effort were required to outgrow the sacred mythologies of Muslim politics in India.

Shakir's capacity for patient and hard work is also beyond doubt. There is hardly any exaggeration to the claim of the blurb that "the author has very diligently gone through almost all the literature - newspapers, journals, books dealing with the Muslim situation in Indian." But did his erudition need the testimony of over 300 references which burden this small volume? Often, it is difficult to make out where the quotation ends and his arguments begin. Nor is it always clear which quotations are quoted approvingly. Why does he need to fortify each argument of his own with the quotation of an authority, which is not always so authoritative?

(Economic & Political Weekly, Vol. VIII No. 38, September 22, 1973)

12

Understanding and Transcending Communalism

The problem of communalism has, not only defied solution so far but, what is worse, also defied a clear diagnosis and grip of the intellectuals. Above all, it defies a standard definition. The term is used more to malign rather than to define.

Communalism is a typically Indian contribution to the English dictionary of politics. Standard English regards it as a virtue. For it means concern for the welfare of the community instead of individual self-interest. In India it has become a synonym with narrow-mindedness, fanaticism, bigotry and hatred.

There must be millions of people in the country who honestly believe in communalism and follow it, whatever definition we may adopt for it. But how can there be a dialogue with them on the merit and demerit of their belief if none accepts this derogatory label?

In fact it is the best means to terminate a dialogue and start a polemical quarrel. For nobody accepts the label. Even as a term of abuse it is far from precise.

The Muslim League of Kerala has, for instance, often been described as non-communal by its coalition partners in the state government on the plea that it was different from its name-sake in the north that wanted Pakistan. The Akali Dal has claimed - the claim was supported by different parties at one time or the other - that it was not communal on account of its contribution to the freedom movement. The RSS, too, has flaunted certificates of eminent secular personalities to assert its non-communal character.

Before independence, communalism was used to contrast it with nationalism. The two terms were differentiated by the priority one attached to one's loyalty to an identity based on a religious community or that on the nation. The terms nationalist Muslim and nationalist Sikh came in vogue in this context, to denote a category of persons whose first loyalty was to the latter category.

It is the use of communalism, in the post independence era, to distinguish it and contrast it with secularism that started spreading confusion. For the two terms are in reality not exactly comparable. While communalism implies identity based on a religious community, secularism as such does not suggest any specific single alternative basis of identity. It makes sense only as an adjective and as plural. Thus all non-religious identities like nation, region, language, tribe, caste, profession and class are secular identities. But in most political discussions communalism is treated in the category of all other sub-national identities; which further blurs the difference between communal and secular approaches.

Again, communalism is often sought to be defined as mixing of religion with politics; which many secularists regard as the most pernicious bane of India's public life. In this context, it is somehow completely forgotten that it was Gandhi who used to make the most potent mixture of the two elements.

What added to the confusion over the debate on problem of communalism is the naive question like "why in spite of the partition of the country, in spite of the industrial development and in spite of the spread of education, communal tension continues." The question clearly implied as if these were the remedies of the problem. But why is it ruled out that communal tensions might have continued not "in spite of" but "due to" these causes?

Character of the Communal Problem

Not much reflection is needed to realize, for instance, how the partition has tangled the communal problem. Every Muslim used to be held responsible for the sin of Muslim leadership that had demanded Pakistan to absolve every Hindu of his obligations to his compatriots. W.C. Smith, the celebrated writer of *Islam in Modern History*, reminds that even an illiterate Muslim peasant who perhaps never had a political idea in his head might be kicked about in his village with a contemptuous sneer: "Why don't you go to your Pakistan?"

Many post-independence causes have, of course, changed the character of the communal problem. Modernisation, the process of which was speeded up after 1947, is, for instance, universally known to sharpen all identities including those based on religion. Revolutionary advances in means of communications, faster and easier travel and explosion in mass media shorten physical and mental distances among members of a community scattered all over the country or even the world. Similarly spread of education and easy access to knowledge generally leads a community to fuller awareness of its historical and cultural roots. Modernisation, in short, helps in creating consciousness of geographical and historical continuity in a community. Development process improves material means of its members with which they can pursue the same objective more effectively and visit religious shrines and congregations more frequently and conveniently. In some cases development leads to disintegration of existing cultural identities and the ensuing vacuum is more easily filled by identities based on religious communities.

Finally, the same trend is further accelerated by measures of democratization, politician and participation.

Modernist Muslim More Communal

Communalism as we generally use the term is the concern of a community about its secular problems. Most of the communal tensions have been the result of controversy over share of various communities in jobs, economic opportunities and political powers. Rarely have theological differences led to communal troubles. It is, therefore, not surprising that Aligarh University and the modernist Muslims spearheaded the movement for Pakistan while Deoband and the Ulama remained votaries of united Indian nationalism. Modern history of Indian politics clearly bears out the fact that modernist rather than orthodox section of the population was more prone to communal politics.

Movement of Muslim consolidation, stretching for almost a century till its culmination in partition of the country, reflected growing divergence in secular claims of various communities rather than any divergence in their religious beliefs. Even the mobilization of almost the entire tribe of Muslim Ulama by Gandhi and use of religious rhetoric by them could not divert the attention of the Muslim masses from their mundane urge for a role in economic and political life of the country. An emotive issue like Khilafat, too, could not sway Muslim emotions in favour of the Congress for too ling.

The fact that religious communities exist in India as distinct groups cannot be denied or wished away. But what needs to be settled is their legitimate sphere of communal identity. What should be the nature and extent of its autonomy? The over-emphasis on oneness of religions, some times, proved counter-productive as minorities apprehend in it a threat to their identity and tended to provoke them to reassert.

Communal separatism, it may be recalled, has, at least partly, been provoked by an urge for uniformity. To respect a religious group because it is same as our own and not because it is entitled to respect despite being different, has also undermined the spirit of tolerance in the country. Uniformity, intolerance and separatism have thus been feeding one another.

There are numerous other reasons which have sharpened urge for communal identity; most of them are, again, of secular nature. Modernization, for instance, is universally known to stimulate a sense of self-awareness among all communities including those based on religion. Revolutionary advances in means of communication, faster and easier travel and explosion in mass media shorten physical and mental distances among members of community scattered all over the country or even the world. Similarly education and easy access to knowledge generally make a community conscious of its historical heritage.

Modernization thus helps in establishing geographical and historical continuity of a community. The development process improves material means of its members to enable them to pursue the same objective more effectively. They can visit religious shrines and congregations more frequently and conveniently. The same trend is further accelerated by measures of politicization, democratization and participation.

This, in fact, is a universal phenomenon. Even advanced countries like the USA, Canada and Ireland and regimented countries like the Soviet Union and Yogoslavia,before collapse of communism, had witnessed resurgence of ethnic and religious identities. Their resurgence on the one hand, and failure of national elites to take congnizance of and respect the emerging identities and their sharply articulated urges lead to tensions.

Growing sharpness of religious, regional, tribal, caste and other ethnic identities in post-independence India further indicates that this is an inevitable concomitant of modernization.

Reaction to Indian Nationalism

The Indian situation adds a few more complexities. Its most outstanding feature is the unique character of its dominant religion i.e. Hinduism, which is not comparable to other religions. Hinduism, as Aurbindo said, is Indian nationalism. It is very tolerant about beliefs and practices of other religions because there is room for all such beliefs and practices within its own fold. This fact reinforces the view developed earlier that doctrinal differences are not the main source of communal tension in India. However, the peculiar nature of Hinduism creates two types of dilemma for other communities. First, they feel threatened more by its assimilative and integrationist character than by its aggressive brand. Second, Hinduism as a religion of Indian nationalism is as intolerant of deviations from its standard of nationalism as it is tolerant at theological level. Hinduism meets other religions not as another religion but as a representative of the ancient and native heritage of the nation and has, in that capacity, acquired the de facto right to set requirements and ideals of Indian nationalism.

Hindu attitude towards the other religious communities is thus determined not so much by their religious thought and practices as by the perception of their loyalty to the country. He would not be found wanting in this respect for other religions but would tend to find others wanting in standards of patriotism. This also used to explain the difference between the Hindu attitude towards religions of Indian origin and those of foreign origin. On this reasoning transnational affinities of Christians and Muslims were supposed to dilute their loyalty to the country. In case of Muslims, India's continued strained relations with Pakistan, which was the outcome of the demand by Indian Muslims, is used to cast an additional aspersion on their loyalty to the country.

Nationalism as a form of religion distinguishes the Hindus from most of the non-Hindu communities. It is their concern for national unity that is the principal cause of their reluctance to recognize and respect urge of minorities for preserving their identity. The attitude of militant Hindus towards minorities is supported by many genuine secular nationalists who, in the interest of strong nationalism, are skeptic about the role of sub-national identities. In a similar way, many liberals including agnostics treat these identities as parochial and hence with contempt.

Thus a religious Hindu, a nationalist Hindu and a liberal Hindu often share their skepticism about the identity of religious minorities. Of course the degree of their skepticism and tolerance varies. Hindu communalism, in this context, is a terminological inexactitude. For it is qualitatively not different from Indian nationalism. The degree, however, matters. Nehru, therefore, defined Hindu communalism as Indian version of fascism which is an extreme form of nationalism.

When fascist tendencies of the majority and excluvist tendencies of the minorities clash, the result is communal tension. But the root cause of the clash is varying responses of religious communities to the concept of Indian nationalism. From the point of view of the minorities, as long as there are monolithic tendencies in Indian nationalism, transnational affinities and extraterritorial loyalties are not distinguished, degree of patriotism of an individual is measured by his religious affinities and the measuring rod of patriotism is sanctioned by religious beliefs of the dominant community, they will scarcely acquire enough self-confidence to contribute their full share to the cause of national integration.

As Hinduism does not owe allegiance to a single book or prophet, Gandhi "found not the slightest difficulty in Hindu circles about evoking reverence for the Kuran and the prophet." But he disappointingly "found difficulty in Muslim circles about evoking the same reverence for the Vedas or in the incarnations." Obviously because Muslims believe only in one book and one final prophet.

Rajendra Prasad, too, expressed a similar disappointment about the Muslims attitude. "It is remarkable," he said, "how by his honest and fearless advocacy of communal unity, he (Gandhi) had enraged many of the Muslims and a negligible few among the Hindus."

Many Muslim scholars have debated respective claims of nationalism and religion on their loyalty. They have also tended to divide humanity on the basis of believers and non-believers, that is Dar-ul-Harb or Dar-ul-Islam. Where should India be placed? If Muslims rigidly and literally follow the belief that Islam is a complete and perfect philosophy covering politics, economics, jurisprudence, social and cultural life and all other fields of human endeavour, should they participate in a system which is not based on what might be considered Islamic injunctions relevant to these fields? The theological question which would influence the degree and form of Muslim exclusiveness in India are linked with mundane question of the role of the Muslim community in the country and its relations with the national identity.

A closer look on the concept of Indian nationalism and the role of Muslim community alone would reveal the nature of what is called the communal problem of India. Instead of the customary Hindu-Muslim angle, it should be treated in terms of relationship of each community with the national identity. The concept ofIndian nationalism itself needs to be liberalized, refined and universalized so as to accommodate and reconcile the urge and interests of diverse identities - territorial, cultural, ethnic and religious - while granting a measure of autonomy to each one of them.

What is the legitimate sphere of communal identity? From which limit of activity communalism starts? How to categorise Jamiat-e-Ulama, an exclusively Muslim political organization allied with the Congress, which valiantly fought the Muslim League during freedom movement? Or the National Conference which mixed politics with religion by launching its attack on the appeal and ideology of Pakistan from the mosques and shrines of Kashmir?

Obviously we have tended to measure "secularity" of a party by the extent of its support to Indian nationalism. We also realize that in some cases distinct and autonomous identities promote greater harmony than full uniformity does.

While conceding the role and inevitability of identities based on religious communities in the composite Indian nation, their limitations in promoting national harmony and satisfying all the urges of their own members should also be recognized.

However, if minorities, in over-reaction or otherwise develop into exclusive political entities, its implications, too, need to be seriously considered. For polarization of Indian politics into religion-based political parties to the exclusion of all other identities would freeze balance of political forces. As the popular support of the parties would be proportional to more or less stable percentage of the community in total population, electoral competition between them would become meaningless.

Again, while such parties might have a role as protest parties, highlighting grievances of their respective communities, they can hardly ensure sharing of power by them; unless there is a permanent and compulsory coalition between them, which may not always work and, in any case, may not leave alternative choice for the people. And a community that is deprived of political power cannot have a sense of partnership and equality whatever concessions it might be able to wrest from a paternalistic government.

Thus while the role and inevitability of identities based on religion in the composite Indian nation should be unreservedly conceded, their limitations as political entities in working a democratic polity and satisfying the interest and urges of their own members should also be recognized. Perhaps it is this specific role of a religious identity as the sole basis of a political party that could be defined as communalism and presents a formidable challenge to India's electoral system and hence its democracy.

Two points are pertinent in this connection. First communalism thus defined need not be synonymous with obscurantism and fanaticism. It implies a plea for reorganizing Indian polity as a federation of religious communities instead that of regional identities. A frank and dispassionate discussion would expose limitations of this approach.

The other point to be noted is that this role of religious identities should not be exclusively discussed in terms of the interest of the community versus the national interest. For its adverse effects on the members of the community itself are no less valid criteria for such a discussion.

No religious community is monolithic. It is diversified-if it is healthy and normal-on the basis of, say, class, ideology and region. If all its members are forced or provoked to join a single party, their legitimate urges will have to be suppressed and their growth thwarted. Regimentation and uniformity help neither the nation nor the religious communities to grow.

Members of every community need an identity. But only a plurality of identities would satisfy this need. Interest and unity of a community would suffer if its members are prevented to join, through fanaticism or otherwise, three more important identities already mentioned viz. class, ideology and region. Trade unions and professional associations are, for instance, vital means for the protection and promotion of material interests of any people in modern times. Similarly ideologies, offer alternative approaches and strategies. Freedom to choose would always be vital for the mental growth of a community.

A Multiple Federation

India is a multiple federation; religious, regional and cultural. Merely religious identities do not exhaust the total reality of India. Nor is any religious identity totally homogeneous capable of representing all the urges of its members. If identities based on religion exceed their legitimate function - of providing a socio-cultural identity to their members - and become contender for political power, they would be suppressing many legitimate urges of their own members, arouse fears and hostility of other communities and strain the principles on which Indian polity is based.

It is in the interest of the members of a religious community that their non-religious urges, some of which they share with other communities should also be satisfied. There are a number of secular identities that can subsume or sublimate a part of the urges of the communal identities of its members. If identities based on religion exceed their legitimate function - of providing a socio-cultural identity to their members - and become contender for political power, they would be suppressing many legitimate urges of their own members, arouse fears and hostility of other communities and strain the principles on which Indian polity is based.

It is in the interest of the members of a religious community that their non-religious urges, some of which they share with other communities should also be satisfied. There are a number of secular identities that can subsume or sublimate a part of the urges of the communal identities.

Religion and region are two important parameters of politics. Pakistan had to pay the heavy penalty of disintegration for ignoring regional dimension of the popular urges. In India, on the other hand, federal system and linguistic reorganisation of States absorbed many a fissiparous tendency. However, the forces of uniformity never gave in easily and continue to threaten national unity. Hence the need to underline the role of regional identities in providing emotional bridges between individuals and the national identity and for integrating religious communities. The latter role becomes significant in view of the inadequacies of Indian nationalism, noticed earlier, in this respect. As regional identities, regional cultures, regional histories and regional heroes are generally not much coloured by standardized Hinduism, Muslims tend to own their pre-Islamic heritage at the regional level more readily than they do it at the national level.

All the manifestations of regionalism are not always healthy. But in most cases, regionalism would remain a lesser evil than communalism. The point of friction that it might generate across or on the border of the region whereas communalism can vitiate the entire body politic within it.

While the role of regionalism in the context of national integration has often been debated its potentialities for secularizing the national politics have not been adequately appreciated.

Ultimately what we call communalism can best be combated by providing non-communal fora for meeting the legitimate needs of the people - a sense of belonging to a community and cultural and political urges. Unless alternative bases of identity are made available mere appeals to shed communal basis of identity would have marginal effect.

Secularism - A Source of Confusion

The notion that secularism as such is an alternative to communalism is one of the greatest sources of confusion on the subject. The latter means identity based on religious community whereas secularism is an attribute of identities which are not so based and in itself is no basis of an identity. Region, caste, class and ethnicity are forms of secular identities, in this sense.

To be sure, the struggle of Pathans (Pushtoons), Kashmiris and Bangladeshis was not for secularism and against communalism as such. They were fighting for the preservation of their regional identities which were being threatened by a movement of Muslim solidarity which professedly aimed at removing all other identities. They never ceased to be Muslims and asserted their Muslim identity as well when their regional identity had been safeguarded or when they were provoked as Muslims. Pushtoons, on both sides of Durand Line between Pakistan and Afghanistan, were threatened by Russian invasion in 1979, Pakistan backed by America equipped them with arms and ideology of radical Islam. The same identity that was an ally of Indian freedom movement thus aquired extremist religious ideology. Similarly Bangladesh, for its own reasons, including tension with India, witnessed, decline of its secular cultural identity and witnessed revival of religious extremism.

Region, though most potent, is not the only secular identity. The role of class in certain situations can be very crucial as it cuts across communal identities. Political parties which deal with socio-economic interests of the people and their power urge can play an equally effective role in achieving the same objective. Professional organizations and academic associations also provide a sense of belonging to elite groups. Whatever be other disqualifications of caste, it did play decisive role in cutting Hindu communalism to size in status like the UP and Bihar.

The so-called nationalist elite who decry all "divisive forces," "parochial" loyalties, "sectarian" groupings in the name of one nation either do not succeed on account of limitations of the approach discussed earlier or succeed by raising nationalism to a high pitch resembling a state of fascism. The so-called modernist elite who decry caste, local traditions, orthodox but innocuous customs, folk mythology, fun and fair often unwitthingly strike at the grass root levels of Indian secularism.

The unity of a country is not inversely proportional to number of identities of its people. Even two identities, if not mutually reconciled, can wreck national unity as well as saw in 1947, when the subcontinent was polarised by only two identities of Hindus and Muslims. Multiplicity of identities, on the other hand, often overlap and check exclusiveness of one another. It must always be remembered that basic urges of the people can never be completely eliminated or suppressed. All that can and should be done is to provide them with socially less harmful (or mere useful) avenues of expression, sublimation and channelisation.

Without damaging the root of society, any attempt to inform its natural and traditional identities with universal and human values would certainly be useful.

(Janata, Vol XXXVII, No.1, Feb 7, 1982)

13

Religion, Communal Identities and Communal Violence

Communalism and Communal Violence in India
By Asgher Ali Engineer
Ajanta Publications, New Delhi, 1989; pp. 344, Rs. 250.

Communal violence is not only the weaker aspect of the Indian polity but also of Indian scholarship. Its growing frequency and intensity defy the riot controlling state agencies as well as the analytical tools of social scientists. A secular Constitution framed on the basis of a long liberal and tolerant Indian tradition, humanitarian instincts of the common man, committed peace activists, concerned intellectuals, not to speak of a powerful state machinery and numerically far larger following of the self-proclaimed secular parties have failed to build up defence against communal violence.

Asgher Ali Engineer, in the book under review rightly argues that the age old theory of communal riots which puts the blame on the British policy of divide and rule or ascribes it to the colonial policy of underdevelopment of the economy "is no longer adequate to explain comprehensively the complex nature of communal violence today". One might, in fact, question his assertion that "the theory had its full validity then". Perhaps even then it had only a partial validity.

Criticizing the tendency to use a simplistic theory or an oversimplified hypothesis to explain away what is a most complex phenomenon, the author attempts to develop a broad theoretical framework, for the purpose. He has indeed excellent credentials for the task. He is not only a scholar of repute, with deep knowledge of religions, particularly of Islam, he has also done a large number of empirical studies on communal riots in post-independence India. His commitment to secular values and objectivity, too is beyond doubt. Study of communal violence is for him, as the blurb says, more than an academic exercise, it is a mission for him.

While developing a macro theory of communal violence, the author also provides for micro specificities on which he has collected a lot of evidence, appended to the book. Perhaps a more rigorous exercise could use this evidence for evolving a coherent and comprehensive theoretical generalization.

The relationship between religion, communalism and communal violence are the basic key to his theory. Religion is, according to him, a force to be reckoned with in India, firstly, because it is a poor and backward country. Secondly, alienated insecure urban people seek psychological compensation through religion. Further, religious operators develop their political links. "The scenario is thus complete for religious fundamentalism to play its political role."

It is not only a poor and backward country in which the role of religion is becoming important. Religion continues to be important in American lives-far more important, as Kenneth Wald notes, than politics. Charles W Dunn similarly observes that "religion has become more important in the lives of Americans as religious issues have entered the political arena in unprecedented fashion".

An American's need for "a sense of certainty and community within the larger society's insecurity and impersonality" {Robert Booth Fowler} must, in fact, be greater than that of an Indian. One must not be either apologetic or seek special explanation for what Asghar Ali calls religiosity of Indians. On issues like family planning, abortion and Darwin's theory, there has, for instance been absolutely no organized resistance from religious quarters in India as is the case in America. It is not possible to find any support in the "cascade of books and articles recently published in America on issues involving religion and politics" {Mark A Noll} to Asghar Ali's assertion that "there is no place for use of religion or religious identity for political purposes as far as the west is concerned."

However, the author distinguishes between opportunist and creative use of religion. He also affirms that religion is not the root cause of communal conflict. Communalism, according to him, is all about secular issues without involving any religious sectarian doctrine. He defines communalism as achieving secular goals through religious channels. He also makes a very pertinent distinction between faith as an ideology and as an identity.

The Muslim League was, for instance, concerned with secular interests of the Muslim identity i e, share in power and employment. It did not at all bother about doctrinal or religious problems of Islam. Similarly the Akali Dal to start with was concerned with secular problems of Punjab or the Sikh e.g, formation of a linguistic state, share in river waters and claim over Chandigarh.

In an ideological or theological sense religion has much less to do with politics in India than it does in the west. Engineer, therefore, rightly argues that neither was the Muslim League led by a 'mullah' nor the Hindu Sabha by a 'Shankaracharya'. But he does not draw a distinction between communalism and fundamentalism and often uses the terms interchangeably. In communal politics, religious doctrines and personalities do not matter. But as fundamentalist trends start emerging, 'imams' and 'Shankaracharyas' are becoming politically relevant.

In analyzing the politics and religion of the two major communities, the author, in order to maintain his impartiality, tries to keep the scales even. He quotes Tara Chand at length to show how much affinity there is between the two religions. He also cites much evidence to show a great deal of intolerance, even brutalities and barbarism committed by the Hindus.

The fact however, is that Hinduism and Islam are not comparable religions; unless the current process of semitisation of the former really succeeds. The attempt to prove the essential unity of all religions as Gandhi and Azad did or find out affinities between Hinduism and Islam, as Tara Chand did, have no relevance to either the communal situation or to the understanding of the two religions. The diversity and range of Hindu philosophical thought-with almost no scriptural authority for socio-political behaviour-sharply contrasts with the precise theological and socio-political character of Islamic beliefs.

Theological and philosophical differences, between Hinduism and Islam are not the cause of any conflict between them. It is due to the blurring of distinctions between Hindu religion and the ancient history, civilization and mythology of India. It is the attitude of the two communities towards nationalism that is the real source of confusion. For Hindus Bharat Mata is the most sacred goddess which is not merely a political concept but also has a religious and spiritual significance. Hindus are tolerant of the religions wanting in their emotional allegiance to the most sacred Hindu gods and goddess and mythological heroes. But not to those who waver in their loyalty to Bharat Mata.

The author comes nearer the truth when he differentiates between religious and political intolerance. But there is need to go deeper into the roots of political intolerance of Hindus. As they are in a majority and as nationalism is almost a religion for many of them, even liberals among them find it difficult to appreciate the urge for a distinct identity among Muslim and Sikh minorities.

Again, the author's attempt to find similarities between majority and minority communalism which "feed and fatten" each other is an oversimplification. For majority communalism trends to acquire a nationalistic fervour and develops affinities with fascism whereas minority communalism trends to be particularistic and separatist. A separatist particularistic brand of Hindu communalism was always a marginal phenomenon whereas it represented the Muslim mainstream and demanded partition of the country; more as a reaction to the assimilative character of Congress nationalism than to the communalism of a non-entity like the Hindu Maha Sabha.

Anyhow the author makes a valid distinction between religious consciousness and communal consciousness. One may not lead to the other. Gandhi and Azad were thoroughly religious but not communal. Jinnah and Savarkar were least religious but communal. Under what circumstances and due to what reasons does one consciousness lead to the other?

The author bases his theory on "dynamics of economic development and social change, accompanying it". The capital path of development, according to him, generates ethnic and communal conflict because it is uneven and accentuates exploitation and injustice. It is truer of the developing third world countries where a sense of primordial identities (caste, communal or ethnic) prevails over class identities. As secularism and democracy are bourgeois ideals necessary for developing a capitalist society, he implies, the problems these ideals are facing are inherent in capitalism.

Obviously the theory was developed before the Gorbachev revolution in the Soviet bloc which demonstrated the autonomy of ethnic and religious identities from economic and political systems and their stronger pull than class identities even in a 70-year old socialist system. And as convincingly argued by Nathan Glazer in Beyond Melting Pot, a developed country like the US is far more congenial for growth of ethnic identities than the developing third world. If economic deprivation and exploitation led to alienation of communities, the Sikhs-almost the richest community of India-would have been the most contented and integrated.

At one stage, in one of the articles included in the book obviously written much later, the author concedes that there is basically nothing wrong with communal identities which must be respected, even encouraged. Assertion of communal identity is a universal phenomenon; both developing and developed countries experience it, he adds.

Alas, the idea is not developed further and its implications have not been worked out. Some of the relevant questions are: What should be the sphere of autonomy of the communal identities? What should be their relation with one another. With other types of identities and the national identity? And above all, when does a communal identity cease to be benign and become malignant?

The author sets store on the role of the politicians to connect the loose ends of his thesis. They, we are told, carefully cultivate religious orthodoxy which in turns is used for promoting communalism and which in turn is used for provoking communal riots. "In the ballot box oriented democracy, they can hardly resist the temptation to manipulate the caste and communal sentiments for winning elections."

The statement, in fact, begs the question. Why do caste and communal sentiments matter in winning elections? If a politician is to remain in business, he must take cognizance of the prevalent sentiments. And if democracy is to prevail, how can ballot box be avoided? In every pluralist democracy parties and candidates are supposed to cultivate and manipulate permutations and combination of ethnic groups to ensure their victory. To expect Indian voters, politicians and the democratic system to behave differently is either utopian or hypocritical.

It is the realization of this reality that makes the author pessimistically conclude that communal violence cannot be completely contained in our society. "We will have to live both with communalism and communal violence for quite sometime to come". When a person like Asgher Ali Engineer -a crusader for and scholar of communal peace-comes to this conclusion, one cannot help feeling a sense of despair.

As the book is a compilation of articles of the author written at different points of time and for different types of audience, there is not only an inevitable repetition but also occasional incoherence. However, piecing together some of his arguments in different parts of the book, it is possible to arrive at a less pessimistic and more positive conclusion.

He has conceded that religion is not the main cause of communalism. Similarly communalism should not be treated as the sole cause of communal violence. It is also a product of the atmosphere of violence which has grown independent of communalism. Further, if we replace the pejorative term communalism by a value neutral term communal identity, it can be argued that recognition of communal identities and proper articulation and satisfaction of their aspirations should be a better way of promoting communal peace.

The author provides another vital clue to the analytical and prescriptive study of the problem when he marshals evidence of the fact that Muslims are a part of regional cultural mainstreams. Locally integrated communities do provide a durable basis for building an edifice of a nation. But the model of nation building that attempts to integrate every community directly with an elusive national mainstream often tends to disrupt grassroots level integration of communities.

It has not been sufficiently realized and Asgher Ali, too, does not squarely face the fact that Indian nationalism is too inadequate a force to unite the nation whereas some of its expressions are a positive threat to national unity. While there are plenty of common symbols at the regional level, they are only a few at the national level. Bhagwan Ram may be accepted as a national hero but is it fair to expect Muslims to worship him as 'bhagwan'. The only way to unite the country is to supplement the appeal of nationalism with common super-national ideals and regional sentiments.

The role of (non-religious) ethnic identities in promoting national unity has not been properly appreciated in India. So is the case with religious and communal identities. They are not only a part of the Indian reality which cannot be dismissed but are also capable of making a positive contribution to national life. Moreover, religion, communal identities and communal violence may be related but are also autonomous.

A study of the inadequacies of Indian nationalism, its relationship with communal and ethnic identities has vital relevance for the future of Indian civilization, Indian democracy and Indian unity. But the task is so complex and daunting that even the best works on the subject do not seem good enough to meet the challenge of the situation. And Asghar Ali's work is certainly among the best.

(Economics and Political Weekly, July 20, 1991)

14

Simplifying Islam

The struggle within Islam (The conflict between religion and politics), by Rafiq Zakaria. Viking, Penguin, pp. 470, Rs 250.

The conflict between fundamentalism and secularism, which started soon after prophet Muhammad, has been a recurring phenomenon in the Muslim world down the ages, observes noted Islamic scholar Rafiq Zakaria. He cites evidence from various ages and lands to prove that "the conflict, in most cases, was decided in favour of the secularists". As in the past, so in the future, "fundamentalists cannot defeat them".

Zakaria makes a strenuous effort to project back a modern phenomenon in order to interpret 1400 years of Islamic history. He is set to prove the supremacy of secular forces in times when the concept of secularism was unknown and unpracticed in any society, much so in a Muslim society. For as the author acknowledges: "unlike Christianity Islam mixes temporal and spiritual and unlike Christ, Muhammad was not only the spiritual but also the temporal leader".

Zakaria pins his hopes on the impact of science and technology under which "the hold of religion has considerably eased". Modern compulsions, he believes, would drive states towards secularization.

Modernization may not automatically lead to secularization. In fact fundamentalism is a modern phenomenon with no precedent in history. Without modern technology, the system that Khomeini was able to build in Iran would simply be inconceivable. A number of factors combined with the process of modernization to produce what has come to be known as Islamic fundamentalism.

Liberation of about forty five Muslim countries from various forms of colonialism and discovery of liquid gold in many of them gave a new politico-economic clout to the Islamic world. Information and communication explosion in the form of TV, direct dialing, email, internet, blogging, jet travel and so on coupled with newly acquired affluence narrowed physical and mental distance between about one billion Muslims scattered throughout the world and made them conscious of their common identity.

Further, while modernization definitely sharpens the urge for identity, it also proliferates identities so that every person has to simultaneously belong to a multiplicity of identities for his fullest growth. Nation (including region), language and class identities might have as powerful an appeal as religion. Nasser reconciled these identities with Islam while the Iran-Iraq war and split of Pakistan are illustrations of failure to do so.

That Indian Muslims got adjusted with regional identities and share these with non-Muslims more readily than they do with Indian nationalism is partly due to the concept of nationalism that we have adopted. Rationalizations of politics and class consciousness are therefore the most potent secularizing influences on subcontinental Muslims.

Religion as a source of inspiration and a basis of identity formation will always remain relevant in politics-but it need not be an exclusive factor in life and politics of a community if it aspires to unfold all its potentialities. It is only in this sense that Muslims need to secularize their politics.

The neat division in Islamic history and society on the basis of conflict between religion and politics (the sub-title of Zakaria's book) is an act of ruthless simplification which lands the author into a number of contradictions. Neither all Muslim kings, rulers, political leaders and caliphs were secular nor all ulama were fundamentalists. Sufis, who were most devoutly religious, were least fundamentalist.

Religion-politics dichotomy which is also spelled out in the book as fundamentalist-secular dichotomy might simplify the study of Islamic history but provides a misleading clue to its understanding.

How misleading it can be is eloquently attested when the author interprets the politics of the Indian Muslims. Throughout the book he treats ulama as almost synonymous with fundamentalists. But he calls Indian Ulama led by Maulama Abul Kalam Azad as secular. He recalls that the premier organization of Muslim divines, the Jamiyyat-e-ulama-i-Hind, was in the forefront of the secular forces. But the author's description of Jinnah as a fundamentalist is the most confused use of the term. For he never sought theological sanctions for his demand for a Muslim homeland. Zakaria confuses fundamentalism sometimes with religious faith and other times with Muslim separatism. He is, therefore, unable to properly characterize the role of either the deeply religious leaders like Maulana Azad and the Ulama who sought validity in composite Indian nationalism in theological terms, or that of modernist Muslims like Iqbal and Jinnah who were concerned with safeguarding the identity and the worldly interests of the Muslims.

Zakaria's contradictions reach an absurd limit when after bemoaning the conversion of Jinnah to fundamentalism, he pays tributes to him, in the context of highlighting the triumphs and achievements of galaxy of secular Muslim leaders of the world, by referring to the fact that "a non-practicing Muslim" like him "single-handedly created the most powerful Muslim state in the world".

Was Pakistan a triumph of secularism or of Muslims? Or a tragedy for both as he implies elsewhere. However, Zakaria's thinking is an apt testimony to his own statement that "no other Muslim in any part of the world is faced with such a dilemma or finds himself as confused".

If non-Muslims are confused and ignorant about Islam and the mind of Indian Muslims, they alone may not be blamed. Zakaria should share a part of the responsibility.

(Hindustan Times 25-9-1989)

15

Theorizing on Communalism

Communal Violence in India by P R Rajgopal, Centre for Policy Research, New Delhi.

Centre of Policy Research sponsored a study on Communal Violence in India by, as its Director VA Pai Panandikar puts it, one of the ablest police official of the country. The author P.R. Rajgopal bases his claim to write on the subject on the fact that he has been "a practicing policeman for over thirty years." During this period, he "have had several occasions not only of handling actual communal riots but also been charged with the responsibility of ensuring the peace at places, which were communally highly sensitive." In recognition of his performance in handling the communal riot in Delhi in 1974, he was awarded the highest police award, the President's Police Medal for gallantry.

The study, according to the author, is drawn liberally on his own personal experience. The foreword attests that "there is minimum of theory and a great deal of hard facts" in it.

However, he does not resist the temptation of trespassing in the field of theoretical generalization on dynamics of communalism "as communal rioting is an integral component of it". In fact it is difficult to find a single "hard fact" which is based on so rich personal experience of the author.

True, communal violence and theory of communalism cannot be divorced. But one need not be over-awed by the credentials of the author in the former field to accept uncritically his judgments in the latter field.

Perhaps only a police officer could have traced communal politics directly to "the democratic constitution which we have given to ourselves" and which has "unfortunately tended to become a very fertile breeding ground for the manipulative politics of the communities and groups."

Rajgopal finds, without any qualification, a positive correlation between communalism and democracy. For "democracy in its ultimate form is a function of numbers and a game of pressure groups."

He elaborates his provocative proposition with a ten page discussion on politics in Kerala - He warns of "the dangers that lie ahead if Kerala example is followed" elsewhere.

What is unique about Kerala? Isn't it a fact that communal riot has not taken a toll of a single life so far in the state? The author does not bother to find out what the North needs to learn from Kerala pattern to reduce recurrence of communal bloodshed.

The other major factor that contributes to communalism, according to the author, is the emigration of large number of Pakistanis and Bangladeshis to India. Are these Muslims returning as a part of some planned conspiracy to fan communal trouble in India? Could growing persecution of Muhajirs, as emigrants from India are called in Pakistan, also be one of the reasons motivating some of them to visit India, temporarily or permanently? Does their experience, which they share with their Indian relatives, inspire a sense of loyalty to Pakistan among the latter?

Largest number of visitors and illegal emigrants, we are told, come to West Bengal. If this be a major cause of communalism, it should be the most communalised state of the country. On the contrary, it has an exemplary record of communal peace. The author, again, does not bother to note it or find reasons thereof.

The point is not what problems legal or illegal entrants from neighbouring countries pose. But the question is whether and how they influence communal relations. The author neither cites any empirical evidence nor any theoretical argument to answer the question.

Instead of treating Kerala and West Bengal as warning signals, a study was needed of the causes due to which these islands of secular politics could survive the rising communal tides all around. For studying causes of communalism, the author should rather have drawn lessons from the states like the UP and Gujarat.

Another issue which the author sees as "a potential cause of communal violence" is that of Muslim Personal Law. He quotes at length a number of what are called progressive Muslims to show that their law is in need of reform. The point should be readily conceded.

What is relevant for the theme of the book is how the so-called backward outlook of the Muslim masses provokes communal violence. There is no doubt that majority of the Hindus resent this outlook of the Muslims. But the question is how far they have a right to impose their views on the other community on an issue, which does not concern them at all. The right is asserted on the ground that national integration demands uniform laws for all communities.

It is mixture of two distinctly separate issues that is the real cause of confusion. The case for reform in Muslim Personal Law is unassailable but for a uniform law is not.

In a way the issue of Muslim Personal Law highlights the central issue of the communal problem viz. How much uniformity is necessary for national unity and beyond what limit it becomes counter-productive.

The author attributes the attitudes and conditions of Muslims to their backwardness in educational field which has "its impact in fuelling communalism" among them. Educational backwardness, according to him, is "due to the fact that they are content with the Madrassa type of education." He quotes a Muslim scholar to prove that "conservatism of Ulama is due to traditional Madrassa system of their education." He believes in "importance of education in bringing into being an enlightened society in which violence will be reduced to the minimum".

There is indeed a strong case for spreading education, particularly among communities like Muslims which are less educated. But the presumption that education automatically and inevitably promotes communal harmony and reduces violence is not so axiomatic. For education also encourages consciousness of fourteen hundred years of the Muslim history and current trends among around hundred crore Muslims spread all over the world.

Past one hundred years of Muslim politics in the subcontinent bear clear testimony to the fact that the movement for a separate Muslim identity was led by educated modern Muslim leaders whereas the Ulama supported the freedom movement and the concept of united Indian nationalism. Again, most riot prone areas are not educationally and economically backward areas but urban and developed towns like Meerut, Muradabad, Bhiwandi and Ahmedabad.

The crucial question of communalism, therefore, is what to do with growing community consciousness, as a consequence of development, democracy, politicisation and education. Would its recognition, as in Kerala, ensure permanent peace among communities? Or can regional identities like that of West Bengal, Tamil Nadu and till recently Kashmir act as a cementing force? Or can identities based on, say, class ideology and party be encouraged to undermine or sublimate urge for community identity?

In general, problem of communalism is a part of a wider question of the role of sub-national identities which are acquiring greater degree of self-awareness as a consequence of process of modernization. What is the legitimate sphere of their autonomy? How to reconcile their claims with those of one another and with that of the national identity?

These questions do not figure in the study of Rajgopal and without them it touches merely the fringe of the problem.

The chapters on case studies of some riots and commissions of enquiry in the book do provide useful information to those who want to refresh their knowledge about them. He rightly doubts "the very utility of such enquiries and their relevance to the understanding of the problem of communal violence and in ascertaining the steps that can help in eradicating it." The Commissions take long years to complete their enquiry and often "touch the peripheral aspects of the riots". Lack of follow up action on their findings "leads one to the conclusion that each of the commissions of enquiry having met the immediate purpose of defusing an inconvenient political situation had fulfilled itself and mattered no more."

The author makes really useful observations in the chapters on the role of army, para military units and police in communal situations. But one wishes that he should not have confined this subject, for which he had ample competence, authority and experience, to merely 15 pages.

His observations on helplessness and ineffectiveness of the army in certain situations, need for better understanding, familitarisation and coordination between army, para military forces and police, existence of a nexus between the police, the criminals and politicians, communalization of police, absence of a machinery for making an ongoing audit and appraisal of the failures, irregularities and improprieties at different levels and in different units of administration, woefully inadequate law and order arrangements in the rural areas which may no longer be immune to communal conflicts and so on are unexceptionable.

He is equally right in warning that communal problem should not be treated as a fire fighting exercise at the level of police only.

The present reviewer also concurs with his conclusion that mutual fuelling of each other's communalism witnessed in the recent past will "set the country on the high road to communal conflicts, the dimensions and diabolism of which will make the past riots seem like trivial incidents."

The concurrence is reinforced after going through the book. For if a person so closely associated with the communal problem, so genuinely concerned over growing communal trends and so liberal in his outlook propounds theories on communalism which are so far removed from realities of communalism, one can imagine how difficult it is to diagnose and treat such a serious malaise.

(Janata, March 13, 1988)

16

Politics of Minorities: Some Perspectives

Politics of Minorities: Some Perspectives by Moin Shakir; Ajanta Publications, New Delhi, 1980; pp. 172; Rs. 60.

Moin Shakir is probably right in reminding us that "the plethora of literature on minorities suffers from many defects." Aside from other defects, he says, "it lacks any rational or scientific outlook." And that "problems of minorities are looked upon in isolation from the realities of the prevailing social and political system." The problem, he argues, is not of getting concessions but of helping in changing the system. For that he prescribes "struggle and struggle alone."

The author is equally dissatisfied with the current definitions of minority'. For him "majority and minority are fictitious entities." From the standpoint of theory, he asserts "no concept of minority and majority is tenable".

The fact that the problem of minorities has evaded the grasp of the analytical tools of scholars and the curative measures of some well-meaning leaders of people does lend some plausibility to Moin Shakir's denunciation of the existing treatment of the subject at the theoretical and prescriptive levels. But in the process he raises rather high expectations about his own thesis. He specifically undertakes to define the problem afresh, put it in a proper perspective, view it in a rational, unbiased and scientific framework and suggest an appropriate political system.

The list of the contents of the book gives an idea of the task the author has assumed. It includes aspects of pluralism, political system, caste and politics, caste and violence, Islam and politics, communal violence, Muslim electoral behaviour and study of the political ideas of Gandhi, Aurobindo, Nehru, Patel, Iqbal and Ambedkar.

The author's knowledge of the subject and his wide perspective are not in doubt. But what he gains in width of perspective is offset by diffusion of focus. The subjects catalogued in the contents are surely not irrelevant. But a large number of similarly relevant subjects have been left out. The whole range of societal and governmental activity impinges on the problem of communalism. Moreover, how could sociological, economic, historical and psychological factors be ignored? And if the influences on the minds of the people are to be counted, the list of personalities quoted by the author is clearly arbitrary.

It is only when one goes through the book that it becomes clear that its scope is confined to the study of some aspects of the problems of Muslims, the Scheduled Castes and Scheduled Tribes. These are called the core minorities, for they share common basic problems like those of "economic uplift, integration, socio-cultural security and end of discrimination."

It would have been fairer to the reader if he were taken into confidence and introduced to the precise scope of the book at the outset. There is nothing wrong in choosing any three segments of Indian society for case studies. But when their common points are stressed, their differences should also be contrasted.

The three segments of the Indian nation chosen by Shakir are not only different in terms of any logic of categorisation but also in terms of self-perception. Imtiaz Ahmad has brought out obvious dissimilarities in the position of Muslims and the Scheduled Castes, based on their different historical backgrounds and socio-economic conditions (*New Quest*, January-February 1980). Unlike Muslims, the Scheduled Castes have no transnational affinities and have no complex of ever being conquerers and rulers of the country. Moreover, being the largest caste of Hindus, they are neither considered nor do they claim to be a minority caste. Again, unlike the Scheduled Castes, the Schedule Tribes are not a stigmatised people; nor do they suffer from any inferiority complex in a socio-cultural sense. They are a proud and sensitive people determined to preserve their identity.

In fact the concept of segments, occasionally used by the author, is more logical than that of minority for the type of treatment of the people he has chosen. But the striking resemblance of the three segments lies in the fact of their being distant from what is called the national mainstream. This is indeed the most vital problem of the Indian nation, whether we view its components as minorities - religious, cultural or social - or segments. The discussion of various concepts of nationalism in the first chapter is therefore very relevant and useful. The author makes the following three major formulations on the subject:

1. Basically the question of national-integration is a fight against all exploitation and oppression.

2. On the constitutional and political plane, it demands more economic and financial powers for and greater autonomy to the states.

3. On the linguistic and cultural plane, it is a problem of implementation of a policy of mass education, by teaching science and technology through the medium of people's languages and by securing rapid economic development on the basis of a planned economy.

The author is, however, quick to realise that "the national integration question should not be oversimplified." But as this subject is not the central theme of the book, the book's scheme hardly leaves him any choice except to over-simplify this problem.

One can in fact read the book with more profit if one does not insist on a coherent theme and an integrated picture from it, but treats it as a collection of broadly related essays.

There are four essays in the book, including one on Iqbal, which discusses Muslim politics. Moin Shakir is one of the most knowledgeable scholars on the subject which he treats with a singular sense of detachment. He deservedly devotes a full chapter to communal riots which "constitute the biggest threat to the secular polity in the country" and their incidence signifies "the emergence of fascist forces." The author suggests the following remedies: (1) inter-communal marriages: (2) ban on cultural and religious organisations dabbling into politics; and (3) modernisation of Hindus and Muslims; and a new economic situation and political culture. Unfortunately, none of the points are elaborated. They are clearly inadequate and simplistic.

Regarding Muslim politics, Moin Shakir makes two significant observations. First, religion has been the unbroken thread of Muslim politics. "Nothwithstanding the desire of a section of the elite for separating religion from politics, the stresses and strains of the situation unfolded the utility of uniting religious faith with political interest." Second, "Muslim electoral behaviour is by and large secular." Muslim support to the Congress is cited as an instance. However, the author is not unmindful of the dichotomy in the two formulations and concedes that "with this process of political fragmentation there is at work the contrary force of social and religious solidarity."

In reality the author overdraws his confusions from Muslim electoral behaviour. Whenever the main contest is between a secular Hindu and a communal Hindu, Muslims would tend to vote. for the former i.e. for secularism. But in case the main contest is between a communal Muslim and a secular candidate - Hindu or Muslim - Muslim electorate behaviour may not be secular. This behaviour thus does not contradict the tendency towards religious solidarity of the community. Both the formulations, in fact, are in need of further refinements and qualifications.

In studying the role of caste in Indian politics, the other main theme of the book, the author significantly underlines its positive aspect. It, for instance, "has been the instrument of mobilisation, a channel of communication, representation and leadership which links the electorate to the new electoral process." The author, however, goes on to argue that caste and other sectarian factors would remain a dominant factor in Indian politics as long as the class character of the Indian state, bourgeois economics and poverty and scarcity of jobs continue. While mentioning the positive role of caste in Indian politics, he might have taken role up the way it could stop the Hinduism wave in some state.

One wishes that the intricate relation between caste, class and poverty had been discussed more rigorously. For growth of class conciousness and rich-poor tensions should undermine caste system rather than sustain it as the author seems to imply.

The third segment of the Indian population which according to the author is included in the core of the minority problem, i.e. Scheduled Tribes, gets barely a marginal mention in the book.

Notwithstanding the shortcomings of the overall scheme of the book and its somewhat imprecise scope, its uninhibited and rational attempt at underlining the problems of the most crucial but alienated segments of the Indian nation is indeed commendable.

(*Economics and Political Weekly,* Vol. XVI No. 18, *May* 2, 1981)

17

Dilemma of Indian Muslims over Bangladesh

A crucial factor that inhibits India's role on Bangladesh is the lukewarm support of its Muslim population. The rest of the country reacted to this fact in two ways. Either it was dismissed as another anti-Muslim canard or it was cited as further proof of the basically treacherous character of Indian Muslims. That the Muslim mind is not closed but is in a ferment, comparable perhaps to the times of the collapse of the Khilafat in the early twenties and of the Mughal empire in the mid-nineteenth century, is abundantly reflected in the Urdu press. But the rest of the Press — as also other forums of discussion in the country — has not much noticed this ferment. At this cross-road of history, the Muslims must not be left to drift into a path that not only takes them away from the rest of their countrymen but also from their destined and deserved status. They must be encouraged to be drawn into an open debate on the subject, expressing their fears and apprehensions frankly and uninhibitedly, and to share in the shaping of the national consensus which in any case needs to be further sharpened.

To be sure, the Muslim reaction to this issue or any other issue is not uniform. A substantial section of the Muslim intelligentsia has reacted sharply and sensibly and is engaging their opponents in serious arguments. Whatever be the size of the respective sections, their arguments are worth listening to.

One source of confusion is the difference between the typical attitudes of the Hindus and the Muslims towards Pakistan at the emotional level. Unlike most Hindus, who have not forgotten the partition riots, the Muslims have no reason to be emotionally anti-Pakistan. Partition had divided many Muslim families. While the part that lives in India may have no intention to be disloyal to the country, it may not be possible for it to hate the country where its other part lives.

Muslim Outlook More Indianised

It would be unfair to prescribe hostility to Pakistan as test for the patriotism of Indian Muslims.

But what puts additional emotional strain on the Indian Muslims in taking a rational and patriotic stand on Bangladesh is the fact that ethnically and culturally they (except of West Bengal) are closer to West Pakistan than to East. Moreover, they are also understandably disturbed over the treatment meted out to the Bihari Muslims as non-Bengali Muslims are called in Bangladesh. These Muslims, who had, by and large, aligned themselves with the regime of exploitation and regimentation were victims of popular wrath. Thus "events in Bangladesh and the part that India played in the break up of Pakistan in 1971 did not find favour", according to K.L. Gauba, "among the Muslims in general". Articulating the general Muslim feelings on the subject, Maulana Abul Hasan Nadvi regretted that, "in a country with a Muslim majority, the idol of language prevailed....... and national and racial zealtory smashed the brotherhood of Islam". Its most shameful aspect, according to him, "has been to arm the enemies of Islam with one more weapon against it".

Nevertheless, Muslims of India were expected by their compatriots to sympathies with the people of Bangladesh, who were victims of barbaric atrocities of Pakistan army out of humanitarian considerations, if not as Indian patriots. Granted that Bihari Muslims, who had aligned with Pakistani regime of oppression and were victims of popular wrath, deserved sympathy but there is no justification for punishing the entire Bengali community for the actions of some of its members. Moreover, the sufferings of Biharis at the hand of the angry masses bear no comparison with the state-organised massacre of genocidal proportions unleashed against the Bengalis. Further, while the Bangladesh government has disowned and condemned excesses committed against the Biharis, the Pakistan government is eulogizing the action of the army.

Many Muslims have argued that support to the regional aspirations of Bangladesh might start a chain reaction in India by similarly arousing regional and secessionist sentiments. This over-nationalistic posture is partly a rationalization of the Muslims' anti-Bangladesh attitude. But partly it is also due to the fact that the Muslim outlook is comparatively more Indianised or subcontinentalist than is that of the other communities. It has not been regionalized and is, therefore, mentally less capable of appreciating the aspirations of Bangladesh.

Those who condone the brutal actions of the Pakistani army on the ground that this was the only way to meet the threat of secession overlook the fact that the demand for secession followed the rejection of the autonomy demand and the army crackdown. Those who suspect the germs of secession in the six-point programme of the Awami League must explain why the army action did not precede the election as the programme had been adopted long before that. In any case, Indian Muslims must be the last to make a fetish of an anti-secessionist stand. For, if support of a large section of Indian Muslims could justify secession of the Muslim majority areas from India in 1947 — even though secessionist sentiment had not been very strong in these areas — surely the demand of the Bengalis to rid of army rule is more justified.

The Muslims who frankly admit that a strong and united Pakistan is a source of emotional and moral strength for them must answer two questions. First, who is really responsible for the threatened disintegration of Pakistan - Yahya Khan and Bhutto or Mujibur Rehman? What is a better way of integrating a nation-

respecting and reconciling regional aspirations or suppressing them and centralizing all authority? Second, what would serve the interests of Indian Muslims better - a united undemocratic Pakistan, purged of its Hindu minority and at war with India, or a friendly democratic independent Muslim country on India's eastern borders? If the Muslims prefer the former position, they are merely providing another arguments to those who want to purge India of all Muslims.

The attitude of the Indian Muslims to Bangladesh would have been far healthier if the Muslim majority State of Kashmir was a more contented part of the country. In the ideological and political warfare which is not an inconsequential part of the struggle of Bangladesh, Kashmir can play a vital role. For it is a test of Indian secularism as well as federalism. The Kashmiri Muslim, is, in fact, in a greater dilemma than the Muslim in the rest of the country. There is a frankly secessionist movement in Kashmir. What should be the attitude of the Kashmiri secessionists to the Bengali secessionists? If the latter succeed, Pakistan is crippled and its capacity to help the secessionist movement in Kashmir is reduced. But if the Kashmiri secessionists support the Pakistan army against the popular uprising, they make out a case for the Indian army suppressing the Kashmiri revolt, however popular it might become.

Further, if the Kashmiri leaders can claim the right of self-determination-including the right to opt out of India-for Kashmir, which has less than one-half of one per cent of India' s population, how can they oppose Mujibur Rehman who wants the right of self-determination for East Bengal which accounts for almost 60 per cent of the population of the country? How can the Kashmiri secessionists condone the Pakistan army's action in punishing Pakistan's 'disloyal' citizens? Surely, they would not like the same treatment meted out to them?

The main argument of the Kashmiri leaders against India's Bangladesh policy is that it is not motivated by sincerity and noble principles. For, the Government of India does not apply the same principles to Kashmir. Apart from manifest difference in two cases, two wrongs do not justify each other. The Bangladesh movement cannot be condemned because India or some other country has committed some mistakes.

This, however, does not mean that the Kashmiris have no grievances. These grievances must be attended to irrespective of Bangladesh. But Bangladesh adds urgency to the task. The least that can be attempted is to seek the support of all such sections in Kashmir as are inspired by the basic values of Bangladesh, whatever be their stand on Kashmir's relations with the Centre.

For a number of reasons, the time for a major breakthrough in Kashmir politics was never so opportune as now. What needs to be conceded is the right of the people of Kashmir to determine the status of the State within India. While the precise degree of autonomy that should suit Kashmir may be debated and may or may not be conceded, the demand for autonomy must be distinguished from that for secession and the right of the people of the state to struggle for civil liberties, fair elections and good administration must be conceded and supported.

We have not perhaps sufficiently realized the healthy potentialities of Kashmir becoming a willing and contented part of India. Selig Harrison was not far wrong in suggesting (New Republic, June 19, 1971) that a solution to the Bangladesh problem lies in Kashmir. The converse is no less true.*

(Economic and Political Weekly, Vol. VI Nos 30-32, Special Number July 1971)

[Formation of Bangladesh did lead to rethinking in Kashmir and their renewed faith in culture based identity. Leadership of Kashmir also lost its bargaining capacity as it was deprived of the support it received from Pakistan after its defeat in 1971 war. The resultant situation prepared ground for a dialogue between Kashmiri leadership with Government of India and finally Indira-Abdullah accord and return to power of Abdullah in Kashmir in 1975. The problem was almost solved till some unwise actions of New Delhi recreated it in late eighties.]

18

Rebuilding Bridges in Meerut after 1989 Riots?

I visited Meerut after the May (1989) riots when the wounds were still unhealed. About 2000 persons had, no doubt, been identified for compensations of various kinds according to a set scale. But the process of recovery was too tardy and inadequate.

What was far more appalling was the fact that hardly any attempt had been made to begin a process of mental recovery. The wounds on minds and hearts of the people were fresh and deep. Nobody seemed to be looking after repairing the social, political, institutional and personal bridges that linked the two principal communities for so long and were blown over by successive riots.

In this "we" and "they" syndrome, individuals have no opinions. They share a community opinion. Facts have no autonomy but are extension of each community's perception of its interest. There are hardly any human feelings for the sufferings of the other community and its losses are discounted. "They might have set fire to their own houses or they have inflated the figures of deaths in order to claim compensation", were the typical callous comments.

In any case, savage killings of innocents were treated as just retribution for the wrongs committed by some members of their community and as proud gains of and legitimate compensation for the sufferings of one's own community.

Each community was convinced that the initial provocation came from the other side. It was then argued that "we could not have turned the other cheek". If the reaction exceeded all proportions, it does not bother anybody. The theory that was gaining legitimacy, implicitly or explicitly, was that every member of a community, including infants and children, is guilty for the crimes of any other member and no punishment was too excessive for that crime.

Another allied conviction gaining ground was that security, justice and punishment were being privatized and one need to look to one's community and not the system to ensure them.

The distrust between the two communities was further compounded by distrust between the Muslim community and the P.A.C., a vital wing of the system, Muslim leaders alleged that most of the killing of Muslims was done by the P.A.C. and not by the Hindus.

On the other hand, the Hindus generally hailed the PAC as their saviour but for which, they argued, they would not have been able to face what they believe was a pre-meditated and well-planned attack by the other side.

Most Hindus were convinced that Muslim mob started the offensive. But instead of condemning the administration for its failure to take preventive and curative measures, to expose the alleged conspiracy and to contain, isolate and punish the culprits, they tended to appreciate teaching the culprit community, not actual culprits, a lesson and to condone whatever means they used. In this way the culprits were better entrenched in their community and they better succeeded in their objective of undermining the system.

In defence of the PAC, it was considered sufficient to state that the initial provocation came from a section of a Muslim mob, which fired on it. For according to the current logic, there need be no limit on retaliatory action and on the culpability of every member of a community for the crimes of others. It is, however, obvious that if the PAC also followed the logic of the crowd, it ceased to be a disciplined police force and an instrument of a civilized system.

The alleged savagery of the PAC in Hashimpura and Maliyana has already been exposed in the press and need not be recounted here. In Hashimpura out of persons rounded up in police trucks, 41 have remained untraced while five were admitted to have died in police custody. In Maliyana, 19 dead bodies were post-mortemed and buried but villagers seek account of another 48 bodies.

Some inaccuracies in the initial lists made soon after large scale disturbances by spontaneous but less thorough efforts were used to ridicule the claims of the victims and confuse the issue; as if burden of proving death lay on those who have been killed and not on those who killed.

Notwithstanding any initial inaccuracies-which were cleared, the alleged crimes of the PAC were so outrageously glaring that no civilized society could condone them.

Thus all those who have a stake in the system and want to restore its capacity to expose and tackle, plans and conspiracies to disturb peace, who want to keep alive their conscience and to preserve a sane and civilized society and who do not believe in guilt by association owed to themselves to welcome a thorough and independent probe into the causes of riots and alleged excesses of agencies like the PAC.

It does not follow that the entire communal trouble in Meerut was the handiwork of the P.A.C. All those who misdirected the mass anger of the two communities were equally responsible However, it is always difficult to determine the precise starting-point of a riot and the real culprit who initiated it. For the gun powder that gathers around over a time is more responsible for it than the match stick that ignited it, which may or may not be deliberate. In such an atmosphere, dividing line between defence and offence often remains blurred. In any case improper and disproportionate reaction is as unpardonable as initial act of offence.

The riots in Meerut started in the early hours of May 19 when a Muslim mob is said to have gone on a rampage against the Hindus of the town following the alleged provocative and tactless way in which the PAC carried large-scale arrests and search of Muslim families.

Most of the 22 Hindus casualties of the riots occurred that day and many of them were uninvolved and innocent.

Those who sought an alibi for the misdirection of the anger of the Muslim mob in the provocation of that day or the accumulated grievances of the Muslims against the PAC or the whole system echo the arguments of those who justify the later massacre of the Muslims and hence do injustice to their cause.

How misdirected was the anger of the Muslim mob is pathetically underscored by the way the only son of Dr. Harpal Singh, the dynamic peace activist and a known friend of the Muslims, was roasted in his car.

When Hindu youth tried to avenge the tragedy by attacking some Muslims, he rescued them with the help of the police. As passions cooled, he walked down to the scene of the tragedy, alone and unarmed, and was greeted by the Muslims with wet eyes.

If similar feelings of compassion and atonement among members of both communities for the wrongs committed on their behalf could be articulated and mobilized, basis would have been found for rebuilding the bridges among the Muslims and Hindus of Meerut.

To be sure, there are far more complexities in the situation. The behaviour of Hindu and Muslim mobs and administrative machinery was also influenced by mutual fears and prejudices, mis-information and rumours. The local situation was further conditioned by overall atmosphere of communal hatred and violence in the country. In short the two communities were separated by a colossal wall of ignorance.

This note does not purport to analyze the causes of the Meerut riots. It merely attempts to find out a basis for rebuilding the bridges between the communities, in their own enlightened self-interest.

In the course of series of meetings that the present writer had with prominent citizens of Meerut, it became apparent that each community was ignorant about urges, motivation and views of the other and that collapse of dialogue between them was not only the worst outcome of the riots but was also the most potent cause of future trouble. Revival of dialogue, it was therefore, felt, should receive the foremost attention.

Accordingly a Committee for Inter-Community Dialogue, with a leading social and intellectual figure of Meerut, Prof. R.S. Yadav as the convener, was set up to undertake this task.

Dialogue obviously implies respect for dissent, a dispassionate view of facts and a commitment to human values and civilized way of life. But more than arguments, sufferings of innocent victims might move many a human heart to realize the consequences of senseless violence.

Unfortunately the relief work-apart from the official compensation for the death of kith and kin, injuries, and loss of movable and immovable property, was done on community basis thus depriving an opportunity of a common humanitarian experience.

Aren't there any people left in the country who can view human suffering from non-communal angle and spare some relief, in cash or kind, for the victims of the riots?

But why is the government so niggardly in its relief policy? Unlike natural calamities and accidents, riots are the consequence of failure of the primary duty of the State to maintain law and order and to protect life and property of its citizens. Full rehabilitation of riot victims should therefore be its moral and legal responsibility.

In fact there is a case for universal insurance of all citizens in what are called riot-prone areas where the state should pay premium and fully compensate all losses. But strangely heirs of a duly insured person by the LIC killed in a riot do not get that much compensation as they are entitled to if killed in an ordinary accident.

It is true that Meerut was a victim of wider communal forces that are sweeping across the country. But obviously Meerut too contributed its mite to the wider conflagration. Likewise, the forces of peace must draw their strength from fight at every ditch. Rehabilitation of Meerut — mental and physical — is a vital part of the struggle to rescue secular democracy in the country. The inter-community dialogue that is being initiated in Meerut must extend to other parts of the country and cover all contentious issues. It is only when civilized channels of dialogue collapse, it takes place through other means and riots is one among such means.

(Vigil, Vol IX, No. 15, October 1-15, 1987)

19

Is Ayodhya only a Muslim Problem?

The form the Ram mandir movement assumed had posed biggest threat to the security of the motherland apart from damaging its international prestige. Forget Pakistan. Forget Muslims. It threatens civilised character of Hinduism and unity of Hindus. It has even divided and weakened the very forces which had gathered together to rejuvenate Hinduism called Hindutva. Did not it threaten unity and stability of the NDA government? By challenging the authority of the Supreme Court and the government headed by the BJP, Ram mandir movement is not only inviting legal and administrative action but also political isolation. By all accounts, it has earned the hostility of an overwhelming majority of Hindus of the country.

Before a dialogue is initiated between Hindus and Muslims as an out of court settlement on Ram mandir-Babri masjid dispute, as is being suggested by many well meaning persons, let there be a dialogue between different Hindu view points on the subject. For nothing would be more fatal for the great Hindu tradition than to impose legitimacy on a group which defies every known tenets of that tradition.

Let us take cognizance of the following broad views held by most Hindus:

1. Many believes that even if Ram mandir was demolished five hundreds years ago to built a mosque, historical wrongs should not be corrected so late. For it would revive endless controversies which would jeopardies present peace and distract national attention from more urgent tasks.

2. Many insist on a proof that Ram mandir did exist at the disputed site and it was actually demolished before constructing a mosque. Services of independent archeological experts and scholars of history may be sought to prove or disprove claims and counter claims on the subject.

3. Many believe that Lord Rama is omnipresent and does not need an extra temple to prove it.

4. Many believe that rule of law and communal harmony are basis of a strong and a civilised nationhood. Hence nothing should be done without clear decision of the court or without goodwill of the Muslim community.

There are many other variety of views held as strongly and as honestly as the group that is determined to build the temple at the disputed land. There is no justification for ignoring view points held by such a large number of Hindus. Finally Ram bhakti is not an essential condition of being a Hindu. Arya Samaj, to whom many prominent BJP leaders owe their allegiance, recognises Ram not as an incarnation of God but only a great man. Some others do not recognise him as a perfect or ideal man and are critical of him, for instance for the way he treated Sita. The attitude of the DK movement led by Periyar towards him is well known.

Nobody has a right to disqualify any such category of people from the Hindu fold. Hindus have never been a regimented and monolithic community and have tolerated a wide range of diverse beliefs. Nor is there any established church which has an authority to pass judgement on religious issues.

However, of late a tendency has emerged to semitise Hinduism; have one prophet as Ram and one mecca i.e. Ayodhya borne out of inferiority complex among a section of Hindus in comparison with semitic religions like Islam, Christianity and Judaism. This imitating zeal may not succeed in adopting good points of other religions but will surely destroy the essence of Hinduism and its distinctive character.

If spirit of tolerance and respect for dissent are an essential and distinctive features of Hinduism, all dissenting views on Ayodhya should be discussed in that spirit within the community. Far more than the Muslim interest and that of the Hindu-Muslim relations, what is at stake in Ayodhya is the fate and future of Hinduism — as a set of beliefs and a way of life.

20

Gujarat: Threat to Muslim Body and Hindu Soul

I had thought, as many other did, that recent tragic incidents in Jammu and Kashmir state followed by a new war like situation with Pakistan would divert the attention of the entire nation away from Gujarat where patriotic upsurge would bury sentiments of communal hatred and violence for ever.

I was wrong when I read few writings in the press seeking justification in recent tragedies of what happened in Gujarat. A letter to the editor asked why have Muslims of India not condemned massacre of 32 men, women and children at Kaluchak near Jammu by the militants. Another asked were the protests over Gujarat louder because the victims were Muslims. One sees a fresh rise in hostility against Muslims in some quarters as Indo-Pak hostility is rising; as if the two were connected. A parallel inter-connection was discovered by General Musharraf who held Hindu terrorism in Gujarat and Kashmir to be responsible for the hostility between the two countries.

One need not be reminded of the questions raised earlier. What is so special about Gujarat? Is it its first experience with Hindu-Muslim riots? Haven't people been burnt alive, children cut into pieces and women raped in riots elsewhere? What are the bonafides of those who are condemning riots in Gujarat? Why did they remain silent over Godhra, where were they when Sikhs were killed in 1984 and Hindus were being killed in Kashmir?

As far as bonafides are concerned, none of these questions apply to me personally. But I am appalled by the underlying presumption of such questions viz one is entitled to criticise the wrongs committed by members of one's community only if he/she had criticised similar wrongs committed by the members of the other community. Why should I compete with any other communities in the number of rapists and child killers?

If sensitive Hindus share a sense of shame and despair over degeneration, dehumanisation and brutalisation of Hindu mobs, how is it relevant to whether they had condemned or not condemned the madness of mobs of other communities..

However, the fact is that every Muslim of any consequences, apart from the secular or "pseudo-secular" Hindus had the conscience and wisdom to condemn the carnage of Godhra and of Kaluchak in strongest terms. But aren't there some Hindus — who can be easily identified — whose condemnation is confined to Godhra and any where else where Hindus have been killed and not to the killings of, say, innocent Muslims and Christians? Do they want to prove that Hindu community can grow without conscience and wisdom? Or they believe murder of innocent non-Hindus adds to the strength of Hinduism?

Fortunately overwhelming majority of Hindus of the entire country have unambiguously demonstrated that they would not allow moral, spiritual and intellectual degeneration of the community to that level. Almost the entire Hindu intelligentsia, entire media — print and electronic —, all political parties led by Hindus, including allies of the BJP and few voices of conscience even within that party, and members of National Human Rights Commission, all Hindus, have condemned the pogrom of Muslims that the Gujarat government unleashed. In it they are joined by international moral intellectual and political forces, media and democratic governments.

What has worried even a Hindu like Uma Bharti is that "inhuman rape and murders of our mothers and sisters and brutal slaying of children has destroyed the image of Hindus being peaceful and tolerant". Gujarat has damaged Hindu image and Hindu character because it has added new murderers and new rapists to the community.

What should further alarm Hindus is that it is adding a new tribe of cowards to the community. After all child of the other community is killed because the killer is afraid that he would be a threat when he grows up.

Such Hindus must be of a strange pathological type who belong to over eighty percent majority of the country which controls almost all levers of power including political power — with not a single Muslim member in the NDA cabinet — all senior posts in the armed forces and civil administration, chambers of Indian Industries and so on.

A community that never lost its self-confidence and refused to be converted — except a minority of less than 15 per cent — during the so called 800 years of the Muslim rule —, a community that could not be converted to Christianity — except less than 2.5 per cent — during two hundred years of the rule of Britishers, who happened to be Christians, has today amongst some people in it who are gripped with a sense of fear that the tiny powerless minorities would some day threaten the existence of the majority of today.

In fact they must be suffering from a terrible inferiority complex vis a vis semetic religions that they are trying to imitiate in what they imagine to be their strong points. They want to monolithise and homogenise Hindus and inculcate in them a temper of hatred, intolerance and violence because they believe these are the characteristics of Islam. They want to create Mecca at Ayodhya and Project Ram to the level of the Prophet of Islam.

Thus they imitiate some characteristic of Islam which are not its essence but give up some essential characteristics of

Hinduism. It never had a Mecca least of all at Ayodhya. Ram is not the sole symbol of Hinduism. It has survived for thousands of years as a combination of beliefs because of its amorphous and evolutionary character. It has influenced and was open to influences by diverse faiths.

Perhaps most glorious period of Hinduism was that of 15th and 16th centuries when through a mighty socio-spiritual upsurge of what are called backward classes, it broke the shackles of ritualist practices and socio-religious monopoly of the elite. Bhakti saints spread the spiritual message through the language of the people and created a renaissance of literature and learning.

Nobody can doubt the influence of Islam on this renaiscance. Nor can anybody doubt that Islam acquired its most creative and cosmopolitan role due to its interaction with Indian philosophies and Bhakti saints.

It is this unique tradition of Hinduism which today stands threatened from what appears to be a fringe phenomenon within its fold.

It is realisation of the magnitude and dimension of this threat and not mere love for Muslims that has motivated bulk of the Hindus to protest against instigation, help, connivance or helplessness of the Modi government over the beastly drama enacted in Gujarat. Gandhi was shot dead for his sympathy for Muslims. But it was his martyrdom that put a new life to the body and soul of Hinduism.

Indeed, the nation as a whole has suffered on many accounts due to prolonged Gujarat tragedy. It was never diplomatically so isolated as on this issue. Its prestige as a leading secular democracy of the world has been badly damaged. One of the important planks of India's conflict with Pakistan is ideological. Trouble makers in Gujarat attempted to weaken its ideological and diplomatic fronts against Pakistan. India's fight against what it calls terrorist brand of Islam loses its justification when it fails to control terrorist brand of Hinduism.

The state and society should indeed be strong enough to deal with those who have committed excesses. There is no reason to be less ruthless in dealing with them if the victims are Hindus. But if the Hindus target innocent members of the other community elsewhere to which the criminals belonged, it is a sign of weakness and fatal to the body and soul of Hinduism.

(Janata, July 14, 2002)

21

The Political System of Islam in Industrial and Post-Industrial Era

What is the ideal political system envisaged in Islam? What political system best suits the requirements of an industrial and Post-industrial ear? How far are the two ideals compatible?

Some scholars underline the inherent inadequacy of Islam in meeting not only the political needs of the industrial society but also of industrialization itself. David Lerner, for instance, observes that " the top policy problem for three generations of Middle Eastern leaders has been whether they must choose Mecca or mechanization".[1] G. E. von Grunabaum asserts that "Islam is absolutely defenceless against the infusion of a rationalist spirit"[2] of the industrial age. Gunar Myrdal, likewise, regards religion in general, including Islam, as a force of inertia and irrationality that sanctifies the whole system of life and work, attitudes and institutions in Asia, and is, therefore, an important aspect of its underdevelopment.[3]

Maxime Rodinson, on the other hand, marshals formidable evidence to prove that there was nothing in the theory and practice of Islam which should inhibit process of industrialisation in general and of a capitalist system of production in particular. However, he is equally skeptic about the role of Islam in evolving a progressive political system for "Muslim religion is monopolized by de facto reactionary elements".[4] He thinks that Islam will be a barrier against the rise of the forces of change, though, he believes that the barrier will not hold.

Before we examine these views about the inadequacies of Islam to meet the material and political urges of the people in the post-industrial age, let it be readily conceded that no religion is perfectly rational i.e. based on merely empirical facts and reason. Nor can a revealed Book be treated as a treatise on political thought and for that matter on other physical and social sciences. Nevertheless, it can be demonstrated that no other religion lays so much emphasis on reason and politics as Islam does.

The Quran proclaims that "Allah particularly detests those who are unwilling to subject their fundamentalist ideas to re-examination"[5]. About fifty references have been identified to the word aql which means "connecting ideas together, reasoning, and understanding an intellectual argument"[6]. Making exhaustive comparisons between religions, Rodinson concludes that" the Quran accords a much larger place to reason than do the sacred books of Judaism and Christinity".[7] Recalling the rational tradition of Islam, Iqbal asserts that "religion stands in greater need of a rational foundation of its ultimate principles than even the dogmas of science".[8] Islam is less deterministic than many other religions. The Quran ordains, "Verily, never will God change the condition of a people until they change it themselves".[9] Islam also emphasizes on the value of knowledge. The Prophet said, "acquisition of knowledge is an obligation on every Muslim."[10] Knowledge, according to him, is "necessary for anyone who wants to do well in this life and in next world".[11] He exhorts followers to "accept whatever adds to your wisdom, irrespective of the source"[12] and to "seek knowledge by even going to China".[13]

It is clear that these saying do not imply division of knowledge into religious and non-religious compartments. The reference to non-Islamic and non-religious sources of knowledge like China- which was a centre of craft and industry and not of theology in those days- shows that "every field of knowledge that is beneficial for an Islamic society be regarded as a part and parcel of religious sciences".[14] Iqbal observes that, "the general empirical attitude of Quran engendered in its followers a feeling for reverence for the actual and ultimately made them the founders of the modern science"[15]. Muslim scholars consolidated and enriched the Greek tradition of science and reason before modern Europe inherited it from them.

Again, the worldly affairs get conspicuous attention in Islam. The Quran not merely says that one must not forget one's portion of this world[16], it also considers it proper to combine the practice of religious and material life.[17] "Economic activity, search for profit, trade and consequently, production for the market, are looked upon with no less favour by the Muslim tradition than by the Quran itself."[18] Ghazali was once asked as to whom he would prefer: an honest merchant or a man who had devoted himself wholly to the service of God. He is said to have replied that the honest man was dearer to him, for he was in the position of waging a holy war.[19] Islam is, above all, a religion of political action. The most visible thing in our religion, says Iqbal, is struggle and power. He believes that power is more divine than truth[20]. A similar emphasis on the value of power can be found in Ibn Taimiyya. Islam, from its very inception, had a political character and its growth was certainly accelerated due to the political power it acquired in many continents. The concept of 'Umma- the Muslim community- is not merely spiritual or ideological but is also political. Maulana Azad observes: "the effect which the words 'nation' (qaum) and 'mother-land' (vatan) have on the rest of the world is produced on the Muslims by the word, 'God' or 'Islam'[21]". Indeed, as a cohesive force, Islam is far more powerful than any other ideology, secular or religious. Common rituals and institutions as well as shared history and culture have further strengthened a sense of solidarity.

Armed with a comprehensive ideology and in response to political demands, Islamic scholars have evolved, over centuries of sustained work, a whole system of jurisprudence which is unmatched in its range and details by any other religion. It covers laws for administration, justice, civil and criminal disputes, economic activities and exercise of authority. Thus a religion that emphasizes the importance of reason, knowledge, action, material needs and political urges of its followers, prescribes a comprehensive set of laws, rituals and institutions and evokes a sense of solidarity among its followers, is eminently fit to build a socio-politico-economic system. The liberation of hundred crores of Muslims from the colonial yoke, the "decision of almost all Muslim States to adopt Islam as their constitution"[22] and their economic transformation (due to oil wealth) has caused resurgence of Islam as possible viable third alternative to Capitalism and Communism. As Anwar Moazzam reminds us that the demand for the establishment of Islamic system was always present and was reflected in the writings of all Muslim theologians and thinkers from al-Ghazali of the eleventh century to Abu Ala Maududi of the present times. But what is significant today is "the adoption of this mission by a majority of Muslim states which have initiated certain concrete steps in the direction of institutionalization of Islamisation process."[23]

The new role that Islam is being tempted to assume is unprecedented in its long history. Muslim empires were not Islamic states in the modern sense. Muslim kings and rulers of the past might have been devout Muslims and inspired by the ideals of Islam but they were not ideologues. Politics always had a fair degree of autonomy from theological control and was influenced by ambitions and temperaments of powerful personalities as also by local geo-cultural realities. The pursuits of Sufi saints and Islamic scholars were similarly independent of the political state. In terms of ideas and practices, there was a vast diversity in the past. Difficulties of communication prevented standardization and the fragmentation of the Muslim world meant that with different choices being made by different governments, the tendencies that were most strongly combated in certain areas could always find a place of refuge somewhere. Rodinson, therefore, emphatically concludes that "Muslim society was eminently pluralistic".[24] However, Islamic world was gradually overtaken by a process of stagnation. This can be traced back to around eleventh century when doors of *ijtehad* started closing. For the last 500 years, Islam, to quote Iqbal, has become "immobile."[25]

Yet Islam did not collapse under the impact of modernization, as predicted by some scholars of Islam and champions of modernization. "Ironically, the process of Islamisation has been initiated by the pressures of modernization"[26]. Muslims did not have to choose between "Mecca and mechanization" because mechanization made access to Mecca easier. Similarly, contrary to gloomy forebodings, Islam did not prove defenceless against the forces of development and change. It was on account of these forces that Islam could mobilize its masses in an unprecedented manner and emerge as a formidable world force. Modernization facilitated communication and standardization. It provided means for regimentation and militarisation. Islam has always claimed to be a total system of life. It was under the impact of modern technology and the modern state that it had become stagnant and monolithic and its political system acquired totalitarian characteristic. Its material and political power increased in direct proportion to the decline in its intellectual power.

Religion is not only closely related to culture and politics; it also influences the growth of socio-economic ideas and institutions. Studies of European civilization have, for instance, acknowledged the impact of Christian ethics on its pace of industrialization and political institutions. Max Weber, also presumes that " the collective mentality of Europe is marked by a superior degree of rationality"[27]. We have already noted the pronounced emphasis of Islam on rationality. It is equally difficult to agree on racial interpretation of Europe's superior rationality. For if it were so, it should have remained manifest in all times. After all, Europe was backward when other civilizations, including those inspired by Islam, were flourishing.

The crucial divergence in the impact of Islam and Christianity on the civilization of their respective regions dates to a time when movements like Reformation and Renaissance (which was partly stimulated by Islam) encouraged autonomy of intellectual activity in the fields of physical and social sciences and literature and Islamic plurality started retreating. With the collapse of *ijtehad*, the distinctive feature of the rationality of Islam and its intellectual activities came to a standstill. As a defensive mechanism against aggressive and the exploiting West, religious straight-jacket on thought processes was tightened. Consequently, massive strides in human knowledge including science and theories of politics, economics and social relations tended to pass by the Muslim World.

Amir Ali, a pioneering and original author of revival of Muslim consciousness in the subcontinent, bewailed that " a follower of Mohammad should abandon his judgment completely to the interpretations of men who lived in the 9th century and could have no conception of the necessities of the 20th".[28]

Apart from the world of difference between the past and the present times, there was hardly any model Islamic polity in history which was in perfect accordance with Islamic laws except the "quasi-ideal period located at the very beginning of Islam in the twenty nine years between the Prophet's death and the victory of the Omayyad dynasty, the period when the community was governed by the Companions of the Prophet and"[29] the four Caliphs. The space and time of this experiment are obviously too short to make it of universal applicability for all lands and ages; more so because there were no written laws in that period. Iqbal further asserts, on the authority of Karkhi, that later generations are not bound by the decisions of the companions.[30] It does not follow that the past is entirely irrelevant in building a political system of Islam for the industrial society of to-day or tomorrow. In fact, it is only recapturing the spirit of early Islam that can reinvigorate it and its modern institutions.

Arguing strongly against the " superficial opinion" that the law of Islam is stationary and incapable of development, Iqbal maintains that change, evolution and rationalism represent the spirit of Islam.[31] Can modern Islam revive this spirit and inform its institutions by it? The spirit manifested in the concept of *ijtehad*, "within the limit of the revealed text, is absolutely free".[32] Iqbal does not believe that Qur'an leaves no scope for "human thought and legislative activity"[33]. "The teaching of the Qur'an that life is process of progressive creation necessitates that each generation, guided but unhampered by the work of its predecessors, should be permitted to solve its own problems"[34]. Even eternal principles should not exclude all possibilities of change " which according to the Qur'an is one of the greatest signs of God."[35]

Iqbal is equally emphatic that hadith should not be used to unduly inhibit independent thinking. He argues that Abu Hanifa, one of the greatest exponents of Mohammadan law who had a "keen insight into the universal character of Islam", made practically no use of the traditions. He adds: "The shari'at values (Ahkam) relating to penalties for crimes are in a sense specific to that people, they cannot be strictly enforced in the case of future generations. He, therefore, "justifies the modern liberals who consider it safer not to make indiscriminate use of them as a source of law"[36].

The crucial role of *ihtehad* as a source of Islamic law has to be restored in order to evolve a politico-legal system which reconciles the spirit of Islam with that of the modern industrial society. Perhaps the greatest weakness of the historical Islam is its failure to institutionalize *ijtehad*. With the expansion of Islam to its present size, it has become exceedingly difficult to hold an *ijma*, the congregation of scholars which has the power of *ijtehad*. Who is authorized to convene an *ijma*? What should be the qualifications of the participants? Should they be merely scholars of Arabic and Theology or also of modern knowledge? But who is to determine religious and secular qualifications?

Abduh was perhaps the first to see in an extended concept of *ijma* the seeds of something like modern democracy when he observed that Government and legislation by the chosen representatives of the people were entirely in harmony with the spirit of Islam. In the sub-continent, the theory of popular *ijma* as the basis of democracy was developed by Iqbal. The transfer of the power of *ijtehad* from individual representatives of scholars to a Muslim legislative assembly, he says, is the only possible form *ijma* can take in modern times.[37] He takes note of the difficulties in a country like India and doubts if non-Muslim assemblies can exercise the power of *ijtehad.* But he does not suggest a way out.

In any discussion of political system of Islam, the relations with non-Muslim nations outside, and non-Muslim communities within, is of crucial importance. The world can no longer he neatly divided into Dar'ul Harb and Dar'ul Islam. In the present complex world, religious entities, cultural entities, economic entities, national entities and political entities are often not synonymous. It may be legitimate for Muslims, whether in a majority or in a minority in a political system, to aspire for recognition of their identity. But their fuller growth would demand recognition of their multiple identities some of which they might share with non-Muslim communities with their own equally proud heritage, entitled for recognition and respect.

It is not easy to find guidance from the scriptures or the history for this problem. That only necessitates revival of the pluralistic character of Islam with a much wider range of plurality in terms of ethnic diversities, institutions and branches of knowledge. With the growth of knowledge, many of its disciplines have acquired autonomy form one another and from religion. Not even the staunchest champion of Islamisation would deny such an autonomy. Not to say, Electronics, Surgery or Engineering, haven't Political Science, Economics, Sociology and Jurisprudence matured by now to qualify for a measure of autonomy?

The question of relation of politics with religion has been discussed dichotomously in terms of their complete separation or integration. Both are unreal options. As long as religion is a community — which by definition it is — and not an individual affair, it cannot be divorced from politics. And the science of Politics cannot grow as long as it remains integrated with another discipline like Religion. Autonomy, in fact, implies overall unity. Within political system itself, the need for autonomy of various segments and institutions is being increasingly recognized.

Just as if a seed is allowed to grow, it blossoms forth into branches, leaves and flowers, similarly the tree of knowledge must get differentiated if it is to grow. It does not imply abdication of religion but ensures it a more meaningful role as a source of inspiration, moral guidance and coordination, apart from its spiritual role. As long as religious urges of the people survive, these roles would be assured as they would not clash with other urges of the people. In Europe, social sciences became independent of religion long ago. The hold of Christianity on the minds of the people, including physical and scientists, has hardly declined. Even in politics, Christian parties continue to play an effective role.

It is not easy to give a categorical picture of a political theory and institutions which would correspond to the ideals of Islam. On the authority of Iqbal one might cite the experiment of Ataturk in Turkey "through whom the spirit of Islam was at work"[38]. Significantly, Iqbal declares, the structure of Islam as a religio-Political system, no doubt, does permit the view that the Turks had taken in accentuating separation of Church and State. The idea according to him, is not alien to Islam. He clarifies the point further by saying that "in the history of Muslim experience, this separation has only meant a separation of functions, not of ideas"[39]. That the common ideology can inspire people working in separate institutions like State and Church is in conformity with the accepted principles of secular politics. This is also another way of describing the autonomy of disciplines referred to above.

On economic matters too, which form the core of the modern political ideologies, Iqbal suggests a similar autonomous approach. Apart from his clarion call to awaken the workers, and not merely the Muslims, in his famous poem, he writes in unambiguous prose, "anybody who aspires to resolve this problem (economic), should keep his mind completely free of all religious and communal differences". For "economic problems that are equally effecting Muslims, Hindus, Sikhs and Parsis eloquently demand that even if leaders of different communities cannot agree on other matters, they should pool their heads at least on economic matters and think of measures for the common welfare of the country"[40]. This analogy can be extended to some non-economic fields also where sections of Muslims might find more in common with sections of other communities than with their own co-religionists. They may be applying Islamic ideas to that field as also other fields and follow an integrated philosophy just as their fellow citizens might be getting inspiration from other sources, Islamic idea of equality, Christian compassion, Buddhist piety, Hindu sense of justice and Marxist concern for the exploited can converge in an autonomous field of activity. It is an opportunity not only to extend field of cooperation with the non-Islamic world but also making Islam relevant and of service to wider humanity and enriching common human pool of ideas and experiences.

Moreover, even a purely Muslim country and even in their capacity as members of the 'Umma, why should the community be forbidden to draw additional inspiration, ideas and knowledge from sources other than their religion? How can a modern political system completely ignore the lessons of, say, French revolution, American revolution, Russian revolution and Gandhian revolution? For this purpose, Islam might have to revive some of its capacity for assimilation and accommodation of diversity. The Theologians, philosophers and mystics (of Islam), Rodison reminds, based their reflections not only on the Qur'an but were also influenced by the Greek thought, Hindu thought and other influences"[41]. Similarly, the great Orientalist, Horten observes: "The spirit of Islam is so broad that it is practically boundless. With the exception of atheistic ideas alone, it has assimilated all the attainable ideas of surrounding peoples, and given them its own peculiar direction of Development"[42]. From 800 to 1100 A.D., says Horten, not less then one hundred systems of theology appeared in Islam.

The theory and tradition of Islam thus eminently equip Islam to meet the needs and challenges of modern industrial society. In sketching the principles of a political system for this purpose, much reliance has deliberately been placed in this paper on Iqbal. It is not because he is a coherent and rational system-builder but because his passionate devotion to the cause of Islam and Muslims should leave no doubt about the bonafides of a system based on his views.

There cannot be any unanimity on what should be the political system of Islam. But it must ensure unregimented growth of Science, Technology and knowledge about human and material problems. It must legitimize the urge and pursuit for resources and their deployment in a planned manner. It must not permit growth of inequalities and exploitation. It must provide opportunities for full human growth-intellectually, physically, spiritually and morally. Power must belong to the people and not to an individual and group. Law making power must rest with their representative. It must ensure right of dissent and freedom of belief. It must permit religious and ethnic groups to maintain their identities. It must allow generation of forces that can counter atomization, alienation and mechanization of human souls. It must cater to the cultural and aesthetic needs of the people. Above all, the system must be informed with basic human values. To be sure, this utopia is not entirely political but the political framework must allow appropriate non-political factors to operate in it.

It may be legitimately asked as to what is peculiarly Islamic about such a system which is just based on certain universal principles of humanity, democracy, justice and similar other virtues. These universal principles were evolved after centuries of struggle in which Islam has made a notable contribution. Just because they have become universal, they need not be disowned by Islam. Moreover, they are far from actual realization and might need a religious sanction for their effective implementation which would re-establish the relevance of Islam. Further, in an equitable political system, which is also in harmony with the principles of Islam, it should feel confident of exerting its influence on account of its rich cultural heritage and its spiritual message. However, the question need not be dismissed altogether. In the past, too, Islam had often to choose between liberalizing itself, assimilating new ideas and becoming a common pool of universal value against maintaining its uniformity and uniqueness. At times of crisis and insecurity, it opted for the latter. At times of self confidence and growth, it opted for the former. While trying to explain the causes which determined the attitude of the 'Ulama in favour of the latter course and finality of schools of Mohammadan law, Iqbal maintains: "since thing have changed and the world of Islam is today confronted and affected by new forces set free by the extraordinary development of human thought in all directions, I see no reason why this attitude should be maintained any longer"[43].

Whether things have really changed or inadequately changed may be a debatable point. But the point has hardly been debated and the debate implies cognizance of the present objective realities. What is being done instead is that rival political theories are seeking legitimacy on the basis of their respective interpretations of the scriptures and *fiqh*. In fact, like all religions-as also great works-Islam does lend itself to diverse interpretations. But in the absence of a theoretical framework, these interpretations can strain the structure of Islam and reduce the entire debate to a semantic polemics which requires more linguistic expertise than knowledge and intellect.

The debate between what are called conservatives and liberals, theocrats and secularists and fundamentalists and progressives would make a limited contribution to the evolution of an Islamic polity relevant to the times as long as it does not outgrow the semantic framework in which it has imprisoned itself. The question of questions is whether the time has come for attempting a reconstruction of religious thought in Islam which makes *ijtehad* a living institution and which provides for autonomy of various disciplines of knowledge. Unless the level of the debate is raised from semantic to intellectual, the process of Islamisation which has admittedly made strides in recent years, may remain lopsided and its software may not be able to keep pace with its hardware.

Notes

1. David Lerner, The Passing of Traditional Society: Modernizing the Middle East (Macmillan, 1958), p. 405.
2. G.E. Von Grunabaum (ed), Unity and Variety in Muslim Civilization, 1955, p.12.
3. Gunar Myrdal, Asian Drama (Pantheon, 1968), p.109.

4. Maxime Rodison, Islam and Captalism, (Allen Lane, 1974), p.233.
5. 8:23, cf 10:100.
6. n 4.p.79.
7. Ibid,p.91.
8. Sir Mohd.Iqbal, Reconstruction of Religious Thought in Islam(New Taj, Delhi 1974), p.12.
9. 13:11.
10. Mulla Sadra in his commentary on 'Usul al Kafi, p.120. quoted in Al-Tawhid, Vol. 1, No. 1, Tehran. Muharran 1404.
11. Al-Nizam al-Tarbawi, fi al-Islam, p.188.
12. Mukhtar-al-ahadith al-nabawiyya wa al-hikam al-Muhammadiyya, p.70 quoted ibid.
13. Al Ghazali, Ihka ulum-al-din, Vol.1, p.14.
14. Dr. Mohdi Gulshani "science and the Mulim 'Umma", Al-Tawhid, Vol.1. No.i, p.117.
15. n.8, p.14.
16. 28:77.
17. 2:193.
18. n.4, p.16.
19. *Ibid*, p.111.
20. Javed Iqbal, Stray Thoughts, p.90.
21. Quoted by M.U. Haq, Muslim Politics in Modern India, (Meenakshi Prakashan, Meerut, 1970), p.132.
22. Anwar Moazzam, Islam and Contemporary Works, (Light and Life, 1981) p.viii.
23. *Ibid.*
24. n.4, p. 101.
25. n.8, p. 107.
26. n.22, p. 1.
27. n.4, p. 77.
28. Spirit of Islam, p.172.
29. n.4, p. 69.
30. n.8, p. 175.
31. *Ibid*, p. 164.
32. *Ibid*, p. 173.
33. *Ibid*, p. 167.
34. *Ibid*, p. 172.
35. *Ibid*, p. 167.
36. *Ibid*, p. 172.

37. *Ibid*, p. 173.
38. *Ibid*, p. 153.
39. *Ibid*, p. 153-54.
40. Tassadiq Hussain Taj, Mazamin-e-Iqbal, Hyderabad, p.101.
41. n.4, p.186.
42. n.8, p.164.
43. *Ibid*, p.168.

(Islam and the Modern Age, Vol XIX, No. 3, August 1988)

22

Modernisation of Islamic Tradition by Iqbal

The either or paradigm of modernity and tradition does not fit on Iqbal. For his "philosophic-poetic genius represents on the one hand, a continuity of tradition and, on the other, an attempt to integrate it with contemporary world-thought, with an intention to set the tradition in an upward direction. Iqbal is unique among the contemporaries of his culture as he combines tradition with modernity with an eye on futurity which in his peculiar symbolism is named eternity."[1]

In fact tradition and modernity acquire a dialectical relationship in Iqbal. Essentially he aims at modernization of the tradition with a view to perpetuating it. He was thus a more effective modernizer and a more faithful traditionalist than many of his contemporaries in the Muslim community.As an individual he was conscious of the continuity of his identity; from his Brahamanic ancestry, and, in his formative stage, of the national and racial Identity. But it would be more appropriate and logical to confine the present study of Iqbal to his final and mature stage when he emerged as the most learned and authentic voice of Muslim identity in India, having given best part of his life "to a careful study of Islam, its law and polity, its culture, its history and its civilisation."[2]

Modernization, as has been universally observed, revives and sharpens various kinds of identities. The trends of high political mobilization and identity formation in the Muslim community, too, can be attributed to modernization.[3]

Without implying value judgement, Iqbal's role in promoting identity consciousness among the Muslims is thus that of a modernizer. One of the attributes of Islam which impresses him is that of identity maker.[4]

This identity was sharpened , in his view, by Islam's confrontation with the Modern West. For he says: "Muslims became Muslims by the stormy West."

Awareness, affirmation and assertion of individual and collective identity are the corner stone of Iqbal's poetry and philosophy. He dwells on religious and secular aspects of these identities. He makes a bold attempt to "reconstruct and revise religious thought in Islam, in particular as revealed by his series of celebrated Madras lectures on the subject, in order to modernize it. One of the important attributes of modernization is change which, Iqbal believes, applies "even to eternal principles." He says: "change is according to the Qur'an, one of the greatest signs of God.[5] If possibilities of change are excluded, the eternal principles "tend to immobilize what is essentially mobile in nature."[6] He therefore regrets "the immobility of Islam during the last 500 years."[7]

In the sphere of law, says Iqbal, "the assimilative spirit of Islam is even more manifest."[8] He does not consider the Qur'an as a legal code[9] and rejects the claims of the 'Ulama' of Islam about the finality of the Mohammadan law. He sees "no reason why this attitude should be maintained any longer."[10] For "things have changed and the world of Islam is today confronted and effected by new forces set free by extraordinary development of human thought in all its directions". He regards the "claim of the present generation of Muslim liberals to reinterpret the foundational legal principles, in the light of their own experience and altered conditions of modern life" as "perfectly justified."[11]

Convinced of the desirability of continuous change in the eternal principles as well as laws of Islam, Iqbal wants to "appreciate he teachings of Islam in the light of modern knowledge."[12] He makes bold to say: It is necessary to examine... what Europe has thought and how far the conclusion reached by her can help us in the revision and if necessary, reconstruction, of theological thought in Islam."[13] He tried to... "attempt to reconstruct Muslim religious philosophy with due regard to the philosophical tradition of Islam and the more recent development in the various domains of human knowledge."[14]

Apart from appreciating modern knowledge, Iqbal wants intellect and rationality to be the guiding factors in the evolution of religious thought. For "in view of its function, religion stands in greater need of a rational foundation of its ultimate principles than even the dogmas of science."[15] There is nothing irreverent, according to him, "in critically examining religious part of human experience."[16] He proposed to look at Islam from the "stand point of the critical student" and follow an "essentially scientific method". He tries to understand the structure of Islam by "eliminating its supernatural elements."[17]

Further, quoting leading modern physicists and mathematicians, Iqbal discovers growing mutual harmonies between Religion and Science.[18] He argues that inductive and empirical method adopted by Islam are proof of its scientific character.[19] The general empirical attitude of the Qur'an, he says, engendered in its followers a feeling of reverence for the actual and ultimately made them the founders of modern science.[20] He therefore, believes that the birth of Islam is the birth of inductive intellect and that in so far as the spirit of Prophet's revelation is concerned, "he belongs to the modern world."[21] He also quotes Biffault in support of his contention that "Science is the most momentous contribution of Arab civilization to the modern world."[22]

Further, Iqbal asserts the reality and importance of the natural world. He says, "Do not say that the universe is without foundation. And that every minute of our life is covered with veil."[23] However, although "Iqbal is philosophically a materialist, he is morally a spiritualist and humanist."[24]

Finally, Iqbal regards *Ijtihad*-independent judgement-to be "the principle of movement in the structure of Islam."[25] He attaches special importance to it as a source of Muslim law, "which, within the limit of the revealed text, is absolutely free." For, "it was permitted even in the life of the Holy Prophet."[26]

Deep analysis of Iqbal's concept of freedom, as elaborated in his prose and poetry, leads Waheed Akhtar to the conclusion that "in his philosophy freedom is the source of all values."[27] This conclusion is valid till we take into account the poet's views in some other contexts. After all he does assert that God refuses to respond to the prostrations of the slaves[28] and the earth refuses to accept the dead body of a slave.[29] He has no respect for those "who follow beaten tracks" but respects those "who blaze forth new trails."

Iqbal's most vital contribution to the concept of freedom is the theological sanctions he provides for it. He links it with the fundamental Muslim belief in the finality of the prophethood of Muhammad. He argues that as the human race has become mature and responsible in its long evolutionary journey, it is no longer in need of divine guidance. "In view of the basic idea of Islam", says Iqbal, "that there can be no further revelation binding on man, we ought to be spiritually one of the most emancipated people on earth".[30] In other words, man has finally been "thrown back on his own resources."[31] It almost means that he has been condemned to be free, as the existentialists would say. Waheed Akhtar may again be overstating his point when he says, "Iqbal's concept of freedom is far more comprehensive than all the existentialist notions of freedom."[32] But it was no mean achievement of the poet to anticipate some of the contemporary existentialist refinements about the concept of freedom and not only to unshackle it from constraints of theology-the greatest of all shackles-but also to bend theology to support it.

Iqbal also shares the existentialist and modern thoughts on the dignity and destiny of man which are a prominent theme of his poetry and philosophy. He accords man the status of an equal partner with God in the act of creation. "If God created the night man made the lamp. God created deserts, mountains and forests, man produced the orchards, gardens and groves. He turned stone into a mirror and poison into an anti-dote."[33] He criticizes the Christian theory of the fall of Adam from heaven which loaded him with a sense of guilt. Man's first act of disobedience, which caused his expulsion from heaven, according to Iqbal, was also his first act of free will, self-awareness and self-assertion which sustained his ego and opened up opportunities for the unfoldment of his vast potentialities.

Iqbal holds "man is a free responsible being." He is the maker of his own destiny. Hence his salvation is his business. The Qur'an, says he, "strongly protests against the Christian doctrine of Redemption as well as the doctrine of an infallible visible head of the church. For these doctrines proceed upon the presumption of insufficiency of human personality".[34] It is eternal and does not come to an end with the dissolution of his body. He regards heaven and hell as states and not localities; so that the possibilities of outgrowing these states, depending upon his actions, are never closed. For "there is no such thing as eternal damnation in Islam."[35]

Iqbal not only condones Adam's act of defiance in heaven but admits his "frank admiration of the devil who reveals a high sense of self respect."[36] It is in fact Iqbal's tribute to non-conformism and dissent.

Another vital feature of his thinking is his spirit of empathy. He candidly admits "superiority of Hindus in point of philosophical acumen."[37] He respects prophets of all religions and calls Ram as Imam-e-Hind. He refers to a number of Hindu mythological figures with due deference in Javed Nama. He not only translated the Gayatri Mantra but had also proposed to translate Geeta and Ramayan.[38]

Let us recapitulate Iqbal's views on religious thought. He believes in the desirability of change, modern knowledge, rationality, empiricism, inductive intellect, science, innovatory wisdom *(Ijtihad)*, free will, dissent, self-determination, self-creation, self-awareness and self-assertion of man and sense of human dignity and destiny and displays an attitude of empathy. Any text book on modernization would list them as attributes of modernization. Indeed as a religious thinker, he seems far more emancipated and imbued with modern values than most of his contemporaries.

It seems Iqbal's religious thoughts have generally not attracted much notice of his community. The 'Ulama' almost ignored or even disapproved them. His correspondence with Syed Nazir Niazi also shows his extreme reluctance to get his lectures translated into Urdu. For, "he felt they were addressed to an audience that was influenced by Western thought and philosophy which Urdu knowing people were not".[39]

To be sure, propagation of his religious thoughts, as expounded in his lectures was not an aim in itself. The lectures seem to be sub-ordinated to the supreme objective of reconstruction and revision of religious thought to meet the modern needs of the Muslim community.

Essentially he is more a poet of Muslims than that of Islam. No theological idea is too sacrosanct for him if it does not promote the interest of the community. At theological level he is flexible enough to declare that as long as a Muslim believes in Tauhid (oneness of God) and finality of Mohammad's prophethood, even staunchest Mullah cannot expel him from the community. But to maintain the unity of the community he would prescribe any number of restrictions.

"Islam", says Iqbal, "has a far greater significance for us than merely religion'.[40] In order to be a live member of the Muslim community, he insists, unconditional faith in Islamic religion is not enough. One must completely imbibe the Islamic culture.[41]

It is his greater concern for the collectivity of Muslims than religious beliefs of an individual that Iqbal seems to make a number of compromises in his theoretical formulations about religion.

While his lectures in English were, meant for English knowing intellectual class, talks of reason, scientific spirit, dissent and modern knowledge, his poetry in Urdu addressed to masses in romantic, conservative and talks of obedience and admiration for power. It fires the imagination of coolest Muslim heads.

As politico-cultural identity of Muslims, their past glory, present plight and future destiny are his major themes, the cool prose (used in Reconstruction) of a universalist, rational and empathic Iqbal gives way to some highly surcharged poetry of a romantic revivalist and crusader Iqbal.

It is hazardous to evaluate his views on diverse subjects by paraphrasing his verse, which being a medium of emotions is less precise than prose.

We have, however, noted that his ideas about revival of Islam were quite liberal. But they were overshadowed by his greater concern about the identity of Muslim community. In doing so "Iqbal mirrored the confusions and contradictions of highly complex environment and there were moments when he could come near the brink of narrow sectarianism."[42]

Iqbal's concept of Muslim culture is less than universal. It is basically territorial and racial. The concepts of the East and the West, recurring throughout his works, imply geographical basis of their respective cultures. "The potentialities of Islam", says he, "lie in the fact that it is a meeting ground of the East and the West - of three continents"[43] Obviously by Muslim culture he means West Asian culture. He nowhere takes note of the contribution of Muslims of, say, Indonesia, Malaysia or Nigeria to world or Muslim culture. His call for unity is addressed mainly to Muslims living from Nile to Kashgar. Within this region, too, he is conscious of geographical, racial, cultural and national diversities. He has not failed to advise

Muslims of the subcontinent "to rid themselves of the stamp of Arab imperialism."[44]

Apart from the apparent ambivalence and ambiguity of Iqbal's views on Muslim polity, Muslim history and Muslim culture, they lack universality, empathy and rationality - the usual attributes of modernization.

Iqbal's conservative ideas on cultural and social life of Muslims are motivated mainly, as are his modern ideas on religious philosophy, by a keen desire to maintain the identity of the community. No people, he argues, can afford to reject their past entirely; "for it is their past that has made their identity."[45]

For further identification of modernizing trends in Iqbal's thought, we may revert to his role in the field of politics. For he realized power of politics and reality of power.

Iqbal occupies a pivotal position in the order of modernist Muslim leadership - from Sir Syed Ahmad Khan to MA Jinnah - who waged a titanic struggle against the domination of 'Ulama' on the minds of Muslims of India between the second half of the nineteenth century to the first half of the twentieth century. Their stress on this worldly aspect of the Muslim life, indifference to theological debates, concern with secular problems of the community like share in the economic cake, and political power, support to modern and technical education, including study of English and efficient use of the modern media inspired a youthful, educated and a non-traditional Muslim leadership which contributed to the modernization of Muslim politics in India. Somehow Indian nationalism could not contain the resurgent urges of modern Muslims which culminated in the creation of Pakistan. What happened to those urges in the new country - which further split into two parts - is another story though.

Nor is it a reflection on the reasonableness, consistency, far sight, integrity, patriotism and courage of the 'Ulama' who withstood the wave of Muslim separatism. Nevertheless they represented traditional version of Islam concerned more with theology than with political power.

Iqbal was convinced that "religion without power is only philosophy." This very idea "urged me to write a Mathnawi about this Truth"[46]

That his conception of power, leads him to reject democracy does not undermine his role as a modernizer. For, most social scientists are of the view that democracy is not as an essential condition of modenisation. Indeed only a modernized and totalitarian set up can implement a sort of total philosophy that Iqbal had in view. Moreover, a part of the reason for his rejection of democracy in India was that he felt it might threaten the interest and identity of the Muslim minority.

However, there are glaring gaps in his totalist approach, which not only detract him from the totalitarian path but also project him as a rational mind.

Iqbal's rejection of Khilafat, a vital vestige of the glorious Islamic tradition, at a time when it had became the rallying point of not only Indian Muslims but also Indian nation, is an act of courage. He pays tributes to Attaturk "through whom spirit of Islam was at work."[47]

He disapproves Pan-Islamism, and supports "the perfectly sound"[48] Turkish view of *Ijtihad*, according to which Caliphate or Imamate can be vested in an elected assembly. He also approves the idea of transfer of power of *Ijtihad* from individual representatives of religious schools to the legislative assembly which is the only possible form Ijma could take in modern times.[49]

Further he declared that "the structure of Islam as a religio-political system no doubt does permit the view" that Turks had taken in "accentuating separation of Church and State."[50] This idea, he adds, is not alien to Islam.[51] He only insists that it should not imply that the idea of the state is more dominant. "In the history of Muslim experience, this separation has meant only a separation of functions, not of ideas.[52] That the common ideology can inspire people working separately in the institutions like the State and the Church, is an accepted idea in modern secular politics.

Finally Iqbal's concept of a separate statehood for the Muslim majority areas was based on a principle of self-determination of a cultural entity of a geographical region. He clearly rejected the concept of Pakistan as a homeland of Muslims of the entire subcontinent."[53]

In economic ideas also, Iqbal takes a non-traditional and non-communal line. He not only revolts against a system of exploitation and disparities but also proposes that "common struggle on economic issues should be kept above religious differences of all kinds."[54]

Thus while Iqbal, in company with Jinnah, took several strides in the modernization of Muslim mind in India, he went further ahead, independent of the Muslim League leadership, in the same direction notwithstanding his several unmistakeably revivalist features.

Iqbal's outstanding success or weakness lies in the fact that he had assumed an ambitious task of attempting to outline a total and integrated perspective of human life, in particular of Muslim community, covering philosophy, metaphysics, religion, politics, culture, economics, ethics and social life. But his intellectual equipment and knowledge about so many diverse spheres were admittedly too inadequate for that formidable task.

The urge to have a view of the whole picture and honesty to appreciate the other side of the picture also contribute to ambiguities and ambivalences in his thought structure. Aware of his limitations as a system builder, he does not attempt a synthesis of his thoughts. As a poet, however, he gets a synoptic abstraction of the reality as he views it. And with a combination of vision, intellect, passion, sincerity and artistic genius he turns his confusions into a raw material for aesthetic masterpieces.

Notes

1. Alam Khundmiri, *Iqbal Commemorative* Volume (Ed), Delhi, 1977, p. 93.
2. *Presidential Address, All India Muslim League*, Allahabad, 29 December, 1930,
3. Yogendra Singh, *Modenisation of Indian Tradition*, Delhi, 1973, p. 81.
4. *Stray Reflections*, Lahore, 1961, p. 72.
5. Mohammad Iqbal, *Reconstruction of Religious Thought in Islam*, Delhi, 1974, p . 147.
6. *Ibid.*
7. *Ibid.*
8. *Ibid*, p. 164.
10. *Ibid*, p. 168.
11. *Ibid.*
12. *Ibid*, p. 97.
13. *Ibid*, p. 7.
15. *Ibid*, p. 12.
16. *Ibid*, p. 16.
17. *Hindustan Review*, Allahabad, August 1909.
18. n. 5, p. vi.
19. *Ibid*, p. 14.
20. *Ibid.*
21. *Ibid*, p. 126.
22. Bifault, *Making of Humanity*, p. 202.
23. *Payam-e-Mashriq*, Lahore, 1923, pp. 85-88.
24. G.R. Sabri Tabrizi: *Iqbal Commemorative* Volume (Ed) Delhi, 1977, p. 38.
25. n. 5, p. 147.
26. *Ibid*, p. 173.
27. *Iqbal Commemorative Volume*, p. 115.
28. Iqbal, *Mysteries of Selflessness.*
29. Iqbal, *Armughan-e-Hejaz*
30. n. 5, p. 179.
31. *Ibid*, p. 126.
32. n. 1, p. 126.
33. *Payam-e-Mashriq*

34. "Islam As a Moral and Political Ideal," *Hindustan Review*, Allahabad, July 1909.
35. n. 5, p. 123.
36. n. 34.
37. Shamloo, *Statements and Speeches of Iqbal*, Lahore, p 69
38. *Iqbal's letters to Maharaja Kishan Prashad*, dated 25 April 1919, and 11 October, 1921, *Ruh-e-Makatib Iqbal*, Lahore.
39. Ibid, p 382, Iqbal's Letter to Mir Ghulam Bhik Nairang.
40. n. 34.
41. Tasdduq Hussain Taj, *Mazamin Iqbal*, Lahore, p. 91.
42. Kiernan, n. 1, p. 48.
43. n. 41, p. 178, Also CF n. 37, p. 198:"Lying midway between Asia and Europe, Islam ought to act as a kind of intermediary."
44. n. 37, p. 11.
45. n. 5, p. 165.
46. Alam Khundmiri, n. 50, p. 50.
47. n. 37, p. 194.
48. n. 5, p. 157.
49. *Ibid*, p. 174.
50. *Ibid*, p. 153.
51. n. 37, p. 195.
52. *Ibid.*
53. Letters to MA Jinnah.
54. n. 41, p. 104.

(Islam and the Modern Age, May 1984)

23

Azad and Iqbal: A Comparative Study

Maulana Abul Kalam Azad and Mohammad Iqbal, the two greatest Islamic thinkers of twentieth century in this subcontinent, espoused radically different ideas about the role of Islam in the subcontinent. After partition, the new states of India and Pakistan appropriated each almost exclusively, and it is only recently that these scholarly monopolies are breaking down and original studies of Iqbal are being done in India. Maulana Abul Kalam Azad and Mohammad Iqbal are, beyond any doubt, two of the profoundest influences on the contemporary Muslim mind of the subcontinent. Their status among the great Islamic thinkers of the century is acknowledged in the rest of the Muslim world as well. Indeed their importance transcends the subcontinent and the century. In the estimation of Shamloo, "Iqbal stands in the front rank of Muslim thinkers of all times,"[1] while according to Mujeedb, Azad is entitled "to a high position among the greatest men of the world".[2]

However, they belonged to two different and polarised Muslim camps in undivided India, between whom there was no dialogue. They are not known to have met each other or exchanged views and neither even took cognisance of the other. Iqbal, who often quoted and consulted contemporary Islamic scholars, never mentioned Azad. Nor did the latter, who often interspersed his prose with the verses of almost all prominent poets, ever quote Iqbal.

The same lack of communication continued between followers of the two masters, and to some extent experts on them, even after partition when each was appropriate by the new states of India and Pakistan in an almost exclusive manner. Iqbal is a father figure of the Islamic republic of Pakistan. Azad, on the other hand, is a symbol, along with Gandhi, of composite Indian nationalism. Muslims in India sought religious and political security in his message and personality after independence.

The emotional and devotional attitude of the Muslims of the subcontinent to their respective heroes inhibited a dispassionable study of their thoughts. Such a study is further handicapped by the fact that Azad wrote in prose while the medium of expression of Iqbal was poetry. The former was more specific and the latter more ambivalent. Moreover, as neither is completely coherent and consistent, it is possible to use selective quotations from their writings in support of one's preconceived viewpoint. Thus, Iqbal has been projected as an Indian nationalist (on the basis of his 'quami trana', for instance), as a Muslim nationalist and as a socialist by different ideological groups. [3] Likewise, Azad's concept of 'wadat-e-adyan' (unity of religions) inspires secular Muslims, while fundamentalists quote his emphasis on the inseparability of politics from religion and some of the Al Hilal (the paper he edited in early life) writings as their main source of inspiration.

There was a definite evolution or change in the thoughts of Azad as well as of Iqbal. The latter outgrew his ardent faith in Indian nationalism after his return from Europe in 1908, when saferguarding and strengthening Muslim solidarity became his principal passion.

In the case of Azad, the ideological journey was in the reverse direction. His early flirtation with the revolutionaries of Bengal, his fits of atheism and infatuation with Sir Syed's writings, are not an integral part of his personality. His regular public career started in 1912 when as editor of Al Hilal, he considered Muslims as exclusive community and wanted them to have a political organization of their own. Later, as leader of the Khilafat movement, he found affinity between his pan-Islamic beliefs and Indian nationalism. Finally, after the collapse of the Khilafat, he emerged as the champion of Indian nationalism.

There is no sudden break in Azad's thought as one finds in that of Iqbal, which the latter explained by saying that his encounter with the west made him a stauncher Muslim. He does not attempt a rigid, precise or coherent philosophy. As a matter of fact, he said, "I hate systems of philosophy; nor do I trust principles or conclusions of philosophy". He was "interested in matters of living experience and not of philosophical reasoning." [4] Azad, on the other hand, insisted on his consistency and asserted in 1940 (in his presidential address to the Congress session) that he stood exactly wherein he was in 1912 (when he started Al Hilal).

Marked differences in their family, cultural and educational backgrounds did influence their overall thinking. Azad did not have any formal education. He was born in Mecca, where he spent his childhood in a family to which "everything western was anathema."[5] His ancestry and company belonged to the celebrated group of Ulama. He traced his ancestry with pride to Maulana Jamaluddin who refused to sign the infallibility decree of Akbar, and his son Sheikh Mohammad who supported Sheikh Ahmad Sirhindi against Jahangir. Qazi Sirajuddin, Azad's grandfather, died in a war between the Sikhs and the Muslims. His contemporaries, most of the Islamic theologians of pre-independent India, organised under the banner of the Jamiat Ulema, acknowledged him as their leader and as "Imam-ul-Hind".

Iqbal, on the other hand, was proud of his brahmin ancestry and his Kashmiri origin. For both these reasons, he had no rigid religious background. He had a formal modern education in the west, including a PhD, and was well versed in western thought. He belonged to the chain of modern Muslim leaders which included Sir Syed Ahmad Khan, Ameer Ali, Mohasen-ul-Malik and Mohammad Ali Jinnah.

The two main schools of thought represented by Azad and Iqbal were engaged in a titanic battle for the minds of Muslims of the subcontinent, which culminated in the decisive triumph of the modernist leadership over the Ulama with the partition in 1947. In a broad and somewhat simplistic sense it may be said that while the western educated leadership was more concerned with the problems of Muslims, the ulama were more concerned with those of Islam. For the former, the identity and solidarity of Muslims and their this - wordily political, cultural and economic interests were more important than theological and religious doctrines. Jinnah won over the bulk of the Muslim community to his fold without using theological arguments or quotations from the Quran. Azad failed despite marshalling scriptural evidence and his unrivalled mastery over religious doctrine.

As Niaz Fatehpuri observes: Iqbal was more concerned with *Muslim* history and conquests than with *Islamic principles* and ethics. He did want that Muslims should dominate over the world again but paid less attention to how to revive Islam"[6] Iqbal's first and daring attempts were at the "*Re-construction of Religious Thought of Islam*" to suit the needs of modern Muslims. Azad attempted to mould the Muslim mind to the requirements of what he considered to be the true Islam. Iqbal draws on diverse sources of western, Arabic, Persian and Indian thought to prescribe a course of action for Indian Muslims. Azad's thought "springs out of the Quran and from no other source".[7] He maintained that "any thought which is derived from any institution of knowledge other than Quran is kuffar and that includes politics."[8]

In essence, Azad's concept of Islam is Quranic while that of Iqbal is cultural. The former defines Islam and the role of Muslims strictly in accordance with the Quran. The latter does not insist on a strict adherence to every letter of the holy book. According to him, "as long as a Muslim believes in Tauhid and finality of Mohammad's prophethood, even the staunchest mullah cannot expel him from the fold of Islam even if he commits blunders in interpreting Fiqh and Quranic verses".[9] But Iqbal prescribes more cultural conditions for a person to be entitled to become a member of the Muslim 'umma'. "In order to be a live member of the Muslim community", he insists, "unconditional faith in Islamic religion is not enough. One must completely imbibe the Islamic culture."[10]

Emphasising the cultural aspect of Islam, Iqbal finds potential in Islam in the fact that it is "a meeting ground of the east and the west - of three continents." [11] His call for unity is addressed to Muslims from the bank of the river Nile to Kashgar. Geo-cultural Muslim identity is thus more important for him than the universal principles of Islam. This concept of Islam as a socio-cultural community excludes Muslims east of India, in Indonesia, Malaysia, etc, and also Muslims living in other parts of the world. For as Firaq Gorakhpuri once pointed out, if people of America and Europe become Muslims, their culture would not become 'Hajazi' culture.[12]

Iqbal regarded pan-Islamism as not only a futile but a dangerous idea. He warned Muslims of India against it, which, according to him, was a British conspiracy to divert their attention from internal political question.[13] He said: "It is significant that in no Islamic language - Arabic, Persian or Turkish - does there exist a phrase corresponding to Pan-Islamism".[14] To call any language Islamic again underlines the cultural concept of Islam. Iqbal like Jinnah did not support the Khilafat movement. He said: "In the abolition of caliphae (Khilafat) which since the days of Omayyads had practically become a kind of Empire, it is only the spirit of Islam that has worked out through Attaturk."[15]

Having emphasised the role of Islam as identity-maker and in the formation of a social, cultural and political community, and having supported the national identities of Arabs and Turkey, Iqbal comes close to the concept of territorial nationalism. But this concept clashes with the universality of Islam and the Muslim community. He has himself condemned nationalism as a shroud of religion.[16] Nationalism, according to him, is a political concept and is not in consonance with the true spirit of Islam. Referring to the dangers of nationalism he said: "At the present movement the national idea is realising the outlook of Muslims and thus materially counteracting the humanising work of Islam. And the growth of racial consciousness may mean the growth of standards different and even opposed to the stand of Islam."[17]

In order to reconcile the obvious contradiction in his stand, Iqbal clarifies that he is opposed to nationalism only when it comes in conflict with Islam and Muslim identity and "claims to be a principle of human solidarity demanding that Islam should cease to be a living factor in the national life."[18] Thus he concedes the legitimacy of nationalism in countries where Muslims are in a majority. In such countries "Islam has accommodated nationalism."[19] However, he suggests a league of nations of independent Muslim countries.

Actually it was Indian nationalism which he had outgrown and rejected, again because it did not, according to him, recognise the identity of the Muslim community. He was ready to stake his all for the freedom of India "if the principle that the Indian Muslim is entitled to full and free development on the lines of his own culture and tradition is recognised." [20] He demanded, in his presidential address to the conference of the Muslim League in 1930, the formation of a Muslim state in the northwest of India, including Punjab, Sindh, Baluchistan and the Frontier Province, which would create a sense of responsibility and patriotism among them. They would, he added, be the best protectors of India against foreign threats, armed or ideological. The foreign influence to which he specifically alluded was that of what he called Arab imperialism, due to which the "civilisation, culture, shariat and education of Islam in India had been stagnated for centuries."[21]

In a logical extension of his stand, he unambiguously suggested in his letter to Jinnah on June 21, 1937 the "establishment of one or more sovereign Islamic states through the division of the country." [22] But there is a vital difference between his concept of Pakistan and that of Jinnah. While the latter conceived it as a homeland of Muslims of the whole country, Iqbal demanded the right of self-determination of a territorially-based Muslim community and advised Jinnah to "ignore Muslims of minority provinces and concentrate on north-west."[23]

Whoever might have originated the idea of Pakistan, it was Iqbal who gave it prestige and powerful ideological sanction. His apologists in India, who deny him this credit (or discredit), are merely denying a fact. What is important for our present purpose is the fact that the cultural concept of Islam cannot escape conceding the validity of territorial nationalism. Iqbal has shown awareness of the fact that while religion is a vital component of every culture, non-religious factors like race, language, customs and environment - usually based on a geographical territory - are no less vital. The area which Iqbal wanted to be part of a separate sovereign state was not only to be a Muslim majority area but also to have a linguistic and cultural affinity, including Ram Tirath and Nanak to whom Iqbal paid poetic tributes. In no case was it intended to be a homeland of all subcontinental Muslims. Javed Iqbal, the poet's son, has pertinently observed, "if Iqbal had lived to see his visionary and vague concept of Pakistan taking practical shape, he would have developed it further to lay the foundation of a concept which could be called Pakistan nationalism."[24]

However, it is difficult to find any guidelines from the writings of Iqbal about the attitude of Muslims to nationalism where they are in a minority. For that matter he does not propound any clear theory of nationalism in states with non-Muslims or mixed populations. While Iqbal's concept of cultural Islam, pan-Islam and nationalism are rather vague and apparently inconsistent, Azad's views on the subject are more categorical and directly flow from his concept of Quranic Islam. In his journey from an exclusive Muslim identity to pan-Islamism and composite nationalism, he bases his stand entirely on injunctions of the holy book. Though he outgrew his emphasis on the exclusiveness of the Muslim community, this community was entirely based on a common faith in all phases of his thought.

Azad's "chief aim was the realisation of shariat and integration of the millat".[25] As the millat in his view has no ethnic, cultural and territorial base, his move from the Al Hilal phase to pan-Islamism was logical. He observes: "Obedience and assistance to caliph is religiously enjoined ('farz') on all Muslims.

Anyone who transgresses the bounds of obedience has thrown off the yoke of Islam."[26] Even after the abolition of Khilafat, he reiterates: "the most important problem is the establishment of the system of shariat of Islam to accept and obey the Khilafat of his time in the same way as obedience to Allah and His Prophet except in matters where the former's instructions violate the injunctions of the latter."[27]

Massive support offered by Hindus to the Khilafat movement had established the compatibility of Indian nationalism with claims of Muslim identity, nationally and internationally. Azad also could not ignore the lessons of the rise of nationalism in the Muslim world. While coming to terms with Indian nationalism, he insisted on its federative character which concedes the distinct identity of Muslims. He pleaded that Muslims should realise "the validity of composite nationalism on the basis of Islam, Shariat and Sunna."[28]

While Iqbal offered no guidance for the Muslims now living in divided India, Azad based his concept of composite Indian nationalism not only on a theological analogy of Prophet Mohammad's accord with non-Muslim communities at Medina, but also on the doctrine of 'wahdat-e-adyan' (unity of religions) which he deduced from the Quran. This doctrine, along with Gandhi's idea of the oneness of Ram and Rahim, formed the theoretical basis of Indian nationalism and the Indian concept of secularism.

Azad did not arrive at the doctrine of wahdat-e-adyan on the basis of a comparative study of different religions but after a deep study of the Quran and its liberal interpretation. He quoted the holy book which proclaimed that prophets were sent to all communities in all ages, and the religions they preached were true. It was enjoined upon all Muslims to show equal respect to all the prophets. As the followers to earlier religions had deviated from the true path shown by their founders, the prophet of Islam came to put them on the right track. The universal message, the Quran says, has been communicated to all mankind. Shariat or 'the path' of rules of conduct do vary from religion to religion. But Azad says, "they differ not in the roots but in leaves and branches, not in the spirit but in the outward form or body."[29]

Further, Azad observed, "The purpose of religion was to inculcate faith in God and lead a virtous life. It is not meant to be confined to any particular grouping of men. Any human being having a genuine faith in God and performing good deeds merits salvation."[30] He went to the extent of making a controversial and provocative statement of salvation. Only virtuous deeds matter. Faced with a hostile reaction, Azad started equivocating and promised to discuss the issue of salvation in its proper context in the third volume of the Tarjumanul Quran, which never saw the light of day.[31]

Azad de-emphasised the socio-cultural aspect of Islam on which Iqbal laid so much emphasis. For him, it was more a set of beliefs than a community. It was not a political community and did not need a separate political organisation. Azad himself was culturally rootless and a perpetual loner, whereas Iqbal belonged to a distinct cultural-geographical Muslim community.

What Gandhi and Azad did not realise was that in India the real problem was to reconcile the claims of different religious communities in the field of politics and the economy and not of religious doctrines. The efforts of Gandhi and Azad in attending to the latter problem to the neglect of the former had therefore little relevance to the situation. Sufis and bhakti saints of the medieval age had resolved the problem of theological differences, but the failure of the nationalist leadership to take adequate cognisance of the non-religious urges of religious communities proved fatal to national unity.

Iqbal gave fuller expression to the political, cultural, social and economic urges of the Muslim community, particularly of the region which now forms a part of Pakistan where he was rooted and of which he was a more authentic representative than Azad, whose appeal was more religious and somewhat other-wordly. Instead of a simplistic belief in the unity of all religious, Iqbal's knowledge of other religions was much deeper. He candidly conceded the "superiority of Hindus in philosophical acumen". [32] He respects and calls Ram 'imam-e-hind'. He refers to a number of Hindu mythological figures with due deference in Javed Nama. He not only translated the 'Gayatri Mantra' but had also proposed to translate the Gita and the Ramayana.[33]

Iqbal respected "customs, laws and social and religious institutions of other communities from the core of his heart". He did not have any doubt that "a communal approach that propagated hatred and defamed other communities was degenerated and degraded."[34] But that did not prevent him from giving expression to Muslim apprehensions about the domination of the Hindu community after independence. Thus he drew a significant distinction between Hindu religion and community. He did not talk of the superiority of Islam over other religions, as Azad had done in his Al Hilal days, but he failed to suggest any institutional arrangement or theoretical framework for sharing of power between Muslims and non-Muslims, as Azad did.

Power is the most important theme of Iqbal's poetry, and power for the Muslim community is his main concern. He says: "Religion without power is only philosophy."[35] He asserts that "Islam is anxious to retain the power to act freely as a constant and undiminished factor in the life of the age." [36]

In Azad's perception of Islam, the most important attribute of God is 'ruboobiyat' (nourishment, mercy and justice), which he bestows on all human beings, irrespective of race or community. It is folly, he adds, to visualise God as a source of fear or terror instead of love."[37] Rejecting the Darwinian law of survival, he says: "among communities survival is only for those which bring beneficence to the world".[38] The contrast with Iqbal's view of the role of power in human history is therefore sharp. Iqbal proudly recalls the expansionary ventures in which the Islamic race (he calls it race as Islam has played the role of identity-maker) had been engaged in for 1,000 years. [39] Azad's interpretation of Quran - and of Islam - is far more humane than that of Iqbal, who relies on the history and culture of Muslims, unlike Azad who exclusively draws his thoughts from the holy book. In his attempt to reconstruct the religious thought of Islam, Iqbal seems to transcend the Quran. He proposes to look at Islam from "the standpoint of the critical student" and follow an "essentially scientific method."[40] He wants "intellect and rationality to be the guiding factors in the evaluation of religious thought" for "in view of its functions, religion stands in greater need of a rational foundation of the ultimate principles than the dogma of science."[41]

In contrast, Azad maintains: "any attempt to prove that religion is in harmony with the theories of science is basically wrong."[42] He argues, "Scientific theories change every day while values of religion cannot be altered now and then to conform to the concept of science." [43]Belief in God, according to him, "is not a product of human mind but is an intuitive feeling of his nature."[44]

Iqbal believes that change applies to "even eternal principles"[45] and without it they tend to "immobilise what is essentially mobile in nature".[46] Azad, on the other hand, believes first, that divine knowledge cannot undergo change as a result of external influences and, second, that whatever changes took place in man's belief led to his spiritual decline: "slowly he began to lose his way".[47] Iqbal, however, regrets the "immobility of Islam during the last 500 years" [48]due to lack of change.

Contrary to this doctrine of change, Azad quotes the Quran: "There is only one path of Din (religion) which existed from the first day and is valid for every age, community and country." [49]He adds: "Din established by God is natural and laws of nature cannot change it."[50] He does not believe in the evolutionary character of Islam. "Instead of evolution," he says, "the law operating in this case is a kind of decline or retrogression." [51] Iqbal refers to decline of Islam and attributes it to lack of change. In Azad's view the decline is due to change or deviation from the original pristine purity of Islam. He holds it to be true about all faiths. They "started with monotheism but later over the years, centuries and millennia they lost their way and deviated to polytheism and idol worship."[52]

Iqbal concedes the autonomy of knowledge of physical sciences from religion and seeks to update and reconcile it with modern theories of physics and mathematics. Azad quotes W Schmidt to prove the "complete bankruptcy of the old theory of evolution in the entire field of nations and human tribes".[53] Douglas points out that Azad has not properly understood Schmidt. The entire discussion, according to him, "shows how superficial was Azad's acquaintance with Western scholarship and how undisciplined his use of it."[54] This could certainly not be said of Iqbal. While in Azad's view there is no scope for change in 'din' and assimilation of new ideas, Iqbal approvingly quotes Horten who says: "The spirit of Islam is so broad that it is practically boundless. With the exception of atheistic ideas alone, it has assimilated all the attainable ideas of surrounding people."[55]

Unlike Azad, Iqbal values non-Quranic sources of knowledge. He does not consider the Quran to be a book of law and rejects "the claims of the ulama about the finality of Mahammadan law". He regards "the claims of the present generation of the Muslim liberals to re-interpret the fundamental legal principles, in the light of their own experience and altered condition of modern life, as perfectly justified."[56] At a general level, he urges "revision and, if necessary, reconstruction of theological thought in Islam."[57]

Reinterpreting fundamental Muslim belief in the finality of the prophethood of Mohammad, Iqbal says, "as the human race has become mature and responsible in its long evolutionary journey, it is no longer in need of divine guidance." In other words, "man has finally been thrown back on his feet." [58]The finality of prophethood is not on the basis of the perfection of the prophet but on the dispensability of prophets, and to prove that "we ought to be spiritually one of the most emancipated people on earth."[59] He further raises man's status as an equal partner with God in the task of creation[60] and does not consider defiance of God a sin. He admits his "frank admiration for the devil"[61] in this context.

There is no doubt that Iqbal was the most emanicipated Islamic thinker of all times who, through the medium of his charming poetry, could exhort human beings, in so many words, to be responsible for their own conduct and reduce their dependence on God, his books and his prophets. No theological idea was sacrosanct for him if it did not serve his perception of the needs and interests of the modern Muslim community. But he had no alternative world-view to guide the human beings thus emancipated. His main inspiration is a vision of the past - Muslim history of conquests and expansion - and not much of the future. He rates power above love and intellect. The alternative of 'mullah' is 'mujahid'. He considers the Muslim community alone a fit instrument of realisation of his objective,[62] unlike the prophet of Islam who considered the human race for this purpose. On account of these limitations, Iqbal "shrank back from the full reconstruction of the value system and institutional system of Islam."[63] Iqbal aspired for and achieved popularity, which limited the quest of his emanicipated personality. He did not want his celebrated lectures on reconstruction of religious thought in Islam to be translated into Urdu and reach common Muslims as they lacked the knowledge he had presumed of his English knowing audience.[64] He promised to be another prophet but "lacked courage and confidence of a Mujaddid".[65]

If Iqbal's vision was limited due to his concept of Muslim destiny, Azad's vision was limited by his exclusive dependence on the scripture. But the latter's vision was certainly more humane and compassionate. He used his creative genius to broaden and liberalise the message of the Quran. He not only aspired to equip Muslims to face the challenges of his time, but also provided doctrinal sanction for Hindu-Muslim unity and the brotherhood of humankind. But he could not match his humanitarian impulse and Quranic inspiration with modern knowledge of the physical and social sciences, in particular of human aspirations, to build up a viable philosophical system and course of action.

The model of Islamic and Muslim approaches adopted in the beginning of this paper to explain the thoughts of Azad and Iqbal, respectively, is admittedly simplistic. For a more rigorous conclusion to the preceding discussion, its limitation should be readily conceded, for Islam and Muslims cannot be contradictory. Notwithstanding the obvious divergence of the thoughts of the two scholar-statesmen, they do concur and supplement each other on a number of subjects and remain within common broad parameters. If Muslim solidarity was the central concern of Iqbal, Azad's concept of the federative character of Indian nationalism implied recognition of a distinct Muslim identity as its component part. If he was proud to be an Indian, he was equally proud to be a Muslim. He was not "willing to give an iota of its (Islamic) glorious tradition of thirteen hundred years." He said: "teaching of Islam, history of Islam, art and culture of Islam, civilisation of Islam are my precious capital."[66] Likewise, Iqbal's very daring theological ventures remained within the framework of Islam. As Pakistan's monopoly over him is breaking, more objective and original studies on the poet-philosopher are being done in India. Ironically, most of the raw and preliminary ideas of the early Azad have become the basis of Islamic revivalism in Pakistan, in particularly of a party like Jamait-i-Islami.

What is history's verdict on the role of the two great Muslim minds of the century? If Muslims had followed Azad's advice, they might have succeeded in getting constitutional and political safeguards of their identity within a united India and would not have split into three parts. If Iqbal's advice to keep the Muslims of the present part of India out of the movement for Pakistan was heeded, they would have been spared of the stigma of having partitioned the country and the subsequent humiliation. If Pakistan had become a laboratory for revision and reconstruction of Islam as visualised by Iqbal, or if it had followed the pattern of a modern secular state as envisaged by its Qaide Azam in his inaugural speech in the constituent assembly of Pakistan on August 11, 1947, there might have been a new hope for the future of Islam and may be of the world.

The ideas of Iqbal and Jinnah to whom the Muslims of the subcontinent gave a chance, failed even without getting a trial, as providence did not give them a chance to live long enough to implement them. Azad was not given even a chance by his community. History's verdict has thus remained incomplete. As the two approaches were neither reconciled with each other nor given a trial separately, their authors left behind more problems than they were able to solve, with the result that one of the greatest opportunities of history not only bypassed Islam but also India.

Only a comparable mind can attempt a fresh synthesis between vision, passion, free thinking and the aesthetic urges of Iqbal, and the logic, humanitarianism and wisdom of Azad; a fresh synthesis between civilisational Islam and textual Islam, between religion and science, between religion and religion, between religious identities and nationalism, and between nationalism and universalism.

Notes:

1. Shamloo (ed), *Statements and Speeches of Iqbal*, p. 6, Lahore.
2. M Mujeeb, *Indian Muslims.*
3. Shorish Kashmiri described him as the Karl Marx of the East; *Chehre,* p. 30.
4. *Eminent Musalmans,* p. 307.
5. Rizwan Qaiser, 'Continuity and Contradiction' in Abul Kalam (ed), *Azad's Religio-Political Thoughts.*
6. *Nigar,* Lucknow, January-February 1962.
7. M Mujeeb, op. cit.
8. *Al Hilal,* September 8, 1912.
9. Tassadaq Hussain Taj, *Mazamin-e-Iqbal,* Lahore, p. 169.
10. *Ibid*, p. 91.
11. Tassadaq Hussain, op. cit, p. 178. Also cf. p. 198. "Lying midway between the Asia and Europe, Islam ought to act as a kind of intermediary".
12. Moin Shakir, *Khilafat to Partition,* p. 109.
13. Mohammad Sadiq, *History of Urdu Literature,* p. 371.
14. Shamloo, op. cit, p. 187.
15. *Ibid*, p. 194.
16. "The biggest among the new gods is native land. That which is its attire is the shroud of religion," Also see "It divides the people of God into nations. It cuts at the root of Islamic nationhood." Quoted by A Beg, *The Poet of the East.*

17. Theodore De Bary, *Sourcess of Indian Tradition,* p. 764.
18. Shamloo, op cit, p. 141.
19. *Ibid*, p. 214.
20. *Ibid*, p. 8.
21. Sir Mohammad Iqbal, *Reconstruction of Religious thought in Islam*, Delhi, 1974, p. 7.
22. Letter to Qaid-e-Azam Mohd Ali Jinnah, *Ruh-i-Makatib Iqbal,* Mohd Abdullah Qureshi, Iqbal Academy, p. 638, Lahore.
23. *Ibid.*
24. Javed Iqbal, *Bikhre Khayalat* (Stray Thoughts), p. 90.
25. Azad, *Tnziat-i-Azad,* pp. 82-85.
26. *Masala-i-Khilafat,* p. 266.
27. *Ibid*, p. 32.
28. Quoted by Rashid-ud-din Khan, *Maulana Abul Kalam Azad, Personality, Politics and Message,* p. 42.
29. Mahadev Desai, *Maulana Azad,* pp. 70-71.
30. *Tarjuman*, 1/384.
31. Ali Ashraf, 'Continuity and Break in Azad's Religio-Political Thought' (unpublished).
32. Shamloo, op. cit, p. 69.
33. Iqbal's letter to Maharaja Kishan Prashad dated April 25, 1919, *Ruh-e-Makatib Iqbal,* Lahore.
34. Presidentia address, All-India Muslim League, Allahabad, December 29, 1930.
35. S Alam Khundmiri (ed), *Iqbal Commemoratiion Volume,* p. 101, Delhi, 1977.
36. A Beg, *The Poet of the East,* p. 321.
37. *Tarjuman,* Volume 1, Sahitya Academy, 1964, p. 2, quoted by Rashid ud-din, op. cit, p. 290.
38. *Ibid*, p. 150.
39. Javed Iqbal, op. cit, p. 72.
40. *Hindustan Review,* Allahabad, August 1909.
41. *Reconstruction,* op. cit, p. 12.
42. KA Nisami, *Maulana Abul Kalam Azad,* 1989.
43. *Ibid.*
44. *Tarjuman,* 1/251.
45. Reconstruction, op. cit, p. 147.
46. *Ibid.*

47. *Tarjuman,* 1/231.
48. *Reconstruction,* op. cit, p. 147.
49. *Tarjuman,* 1. p. 431.
50. *Ibid*, p. 420.
51. *Ibid*, p. 231.
52. *Ibid.*
53. *Tarjuman.*
54. IH Douglas, *Abul Kalam Azad: An intellectual and religious biography,* p. 202.
55. *Reconstruction,* op. cit, p. 162.
56. *Tarjuman,* p. 431.
57. *Ibid*, p. 420.
58. *Ibid*, p. 231.
59. *Reconstruction,* op. cit, p. 179.
60. *Tarjuman,* p. 231.
61. *Hindustan Review,* July 1909.
62. *Tassadaq,* Hussain Taj, op. cit, p. 71.
63. A Jamal Khawaja, *The Muslim Situation in India,* Iqbal A Ansari (ed), p. 259.
64. Iqbal's letter to Mir Ghulam Bheek Nairang, October 6, 1931, *Ruh Makatib Iqbal,* op. cit, p. 268.
65. Moin Shakir, *From Khilafat to Partition,* p. 121.
66. Malik Ram (ed), *Khutabat-i-Azad,* 1974, p. 269.

(Economic & Political Weekly, Vol XXXI, No. 10, March 9, 1996)

Index